MW01154667

The

Spiritual

Heart

Ramaji

Books By Ramaji

No Mind No Problem

Waking Up As Awareness

You Are Everything

The Tao Of Non-Doing

Warning From Kali 2013

The Spiritual Heart

Dialogs on Self-Inquiry, Non-Duality, Tantra, Kundalini and the Heart on the Right

By

Ramaji

The Spiritual Heart

ISBN: 1484944461
ISBN-13: 978-1484944462

Ramaji.org

Ramaji Books
San Diego, California
Email: satsangwithramaji@gmail.com

Acknowledgements

I must first acknowledge my parents. They were my first gurus.

By living a profoundly moral and ethical life, they demonstrated to me by their example the foundation of the way. Later on when things got tough and I was overwhelmed by doubt, I recalled their profound sacrifices in the name of love and my faith was restored.

Next I want to thank Sri Ramesh Balsekar. My biological father was my first spiritual father. Ramesh was my second spiritual father. Because he blasted me with Grace, this book became possible. Jai Guru Dev!

Back in the 1980s, Venerable Shinzen Young helped me to get my feet firmly established on the path of meditation. I was extremely fortunate to know him at a time when I could access his wisdom weekly for the price of a Thai lunch for two in downtown L.A.

Divine Mother in the form of Kali Ma has been running my life for decades now. It is good to ride through life knowing that She is at the wheel. When God is driving, I am happy to take the back seat.

I have had too many spiritual teachers to list here, so please accept my apology in advance if I have not mentioned you. The Teachings and Presence of the towering spiritual giants Sri Nisargadatta Maharaj and Sri Ramana Maharshi have been of enormous importance to my spiritual journey. Their concrete and practical meditation instructions enabled me to finally know who I am.

I am deeply grateful to B.D., Jerry B. Miko, Stuart Baker and Andrew Lynn for their frank feedback and help with the editing. Their insights were invaluable and greatly improved this book.

Finally, I must acknowledge Linda, my wife of 11 years. She has firmly supported me and my journey as a teacher in ways I did not know I would need. Not only that, she makes me laugh every day.

Table of Contents

Introduction

These early dialogs with Ramaji are direct and to the point. The modern Advaita and non-duality community has largely neglected the master technique of Self-inquiry provided by the undisputed great Sage, Sri Ramana Maharshi. Ramaji would like to remedy that.

Aligned by destiny and joy with first Ramesh and then Ramana, Ramaji speaks from his own experience with this most ancient of spiritual paths, Self-inquiry ("Who am I?"). He addresses the hopes, fears and fantasies of spiritual seekers and redirects his listeners to the reality that spiritual realization requires hard work, dedication and earnest effort.

Emergence into non-dual awareness is the beginning, not the end, of a profound journey into the depths of spiritual Self-realization. The great Quest is not completed until, in the words of Sri Ramana Maharshi, "There is only the Self." Then even apparent oneness is transcended.

Ramaji received Grace from Ramesh Balsekar in Fall, 1989. This led to an uncoiling of the mind and letting go at the deepest levels. Awakening followed in 1992 in San Diego.

Ramaji cuts through to the truth with surgical precision in the spirit of his late Advaita guru Ramesh Balsekar and his divine salvatrix, Kali Ma. Ever since Kali spoke to him in 1982 in the meditation hall at the Vedanta Temple Society in Hollywood, California, the great Hindu goddess of ego death and liberation has guided his personal and spiritual life.

Topics covered include how to dissolve the ego (I-thought), the role of Kundalini and the Heart on the right in enlightenment, the "I am the body" thought, non-doership, living in the natural state, non-dual intimate relationships, Tantric Advaita, the art and practice of Self-inquiry meditation, the power of Grace and the significance of the thought-free state.

These Satsang talks, informal dialogs and spontaneous exchanges have been collected, transcribed, reconstructed and edited from private meetings with individuals and small groups in Los Angeles, San Diego, Palm Springs, Santa Barbara and San Francisco, California, Portland, Oregon, Las Vegas, Nevada and Toronto, Canada. Ramaji led his first non-dual retreat in Toronto in 1994.

These mostly casual conversations with spiritual seekers took place from Summer, 1994 to Spring, 2012. Responding to a direct divine command to make himself available, Ramaji moved to San Diego and began his public mission as a spiritual teacher in June, 2012.

Journey to the Heart of Truth

"My teacher told me to hold on to the sense 'I am' tenaciously and not to swerve from it even for a moment... This brought an end to the mind; in the stillness of the mind I saw myself as I am — unbound. I simply followed (my teacher's) instruction which was to focus the mind on pure being 'I am', and stay in it." (1)

— *Sri Nisargadatta Maharaj*

When I was 16 years old and living in a suburb of Los Angeles, California, I had a lucid dream that changed my life. In this dream, I was in India. I was with a yoga guru who spoke to me in Sanskrit. He took me through many hatha yoga postures, then I ended up sitting in padmasana, in lotus posture.

Then next thing that happened was literally mind-blowing. Everything exploded and my sense of separate self that I had been feeling in the dream dissolved totally and completely into a blissful peaceful Ocean of White Light.

When I woke up the next morning, my Kundalini was awakened. I also had amazing psychic powers. I'm not going to go into details, but I will say having this sudden unexpected Kundalini awakening was very difficult. It was hard enough just being a teenager. The extremes of emotion from the Kundalini were astonishing.

I managed to muddle my way through this crisis. I was in high school. I was still living with my parents. Though I knew next to nothing about yoga, meditation or Eastern religion, I knew that enlightenment was real and that it was better than anything else.

I had a reading by a gifted spiritual psychic. She told me that I would have to wait a long time. She predicted that I would not see fruition of my spiritual yearnings until my 40s or 50s. She said I would have to be very patient.

It turned out she was right. To a teenager, waiting for the fulfillment of your heart's desire until you're 40 or so sounds like an eternity. Yet I sensed this delay was in my destiny.

What this experience did is force me to recalibrate everything in my inquisitive young life. Now life was transparent. It was just going through the motions. All the usual things that a young man could get excited about didn't amount to a hill of beans.

I had experienced a blissful transcendental Light that made everything else meaningless. All that life offered was now nonsense. Life was a cosmic joke, but I didn't know the punchline.

It was a paradoxical situation. It made me laugh. It made me cry. It made me doubt God. It made me love God. But one thing was for sure. I could never go back.

In the 1970s, I got involved with some marginal gurus. I made mistakes and I learned from them. I became a vegetarian. I started doing hatha yoga every morning.

In the early 1980s, I ended up living in a Sivananda ashram in Hollywood, California. It was there that my spiritual practice began to stabilize. The assistant head of the yoga center was studying Vipassana meditation. I learned about it from her.

I took up Vipassana ("Insight") meditation in earnest. I would meditate one or two hours a day plus practice mindfulness while walking and when I made tactile contract with something during the day out in the world. The kind of Vipassana that I studied focused on fleeting body sensations. To be specific, on detecting the impermanence in these ever changing body sensations. This became possible when concentration was built up.

I had the good fortune to study with the Venerable Shinzen Young. He is a wonderful human being and a brilliant enlightened spiritual teacher. He has achieved much success as a meditation master. His success is well-deserved.

Even though he taught a contemporary approach based on science, I was drawn to the classic Buddhist text *Vishuddimagga* (Path of Purification). I studied it and learned about the classical stages of the unfolding of impermanence.

This traditional sequence of spiritual events or milestones on the road to Nibbana (Nirvana) is described by a few modern Vipassana teachers, too.

As it turned out, even though I was living in a huge Western city, I went through these stages exactly as described in this book.
These stages culminated precisely as the old book had predicted in the flash of Nirvana. I was doing walking meditation on a driveway in the back of the meditation retreat house in downtown Los Angeles when it happened.

Since Vipassana had been good to me, I stuck with it for seven years. But there came a time when it began to feel restrictive and limiting. There was not anything "wrong" with it. It is a brilliant practice. My clock of destiny was ticking. It was time to move on.

Advaita and Vipassana totally agree on the universal factor of impermanence as being key ("Anicca" in Pali). Vipassana is the Buddha's version of Self-inquiry meditation.

I was deep into my Vipassana meditation lifestyle when I met Kali at the Sri Ramakrishna Advaita Vedanta Temple in Hollywood, California. I was meditating there and the statue of Kali they keep up at the front moved. I saw Her walk by. Then I smelled the most lovely fragrance of sandalwood. Then She started talking to me.

Mother Kali has a very distinct way of talking. She talks like she is in total command, like she is the general and you are the private. She said to me, "You are mine. I own you. Your body is mine. I am in control of your destiny."

I was surprisingly at ease with the sudden turn of events. In my mind, I calmly replied "Okay, I believe you. If that is true, then what is next?"

Whispering in my ear again, Kali added "If you agree to this spiritual contract with me, then I will completely fulfill my side of the bargain. I can guarantee that you will attain spiritual liberation in this lifetime. You must be willing to surrender unconditionally to me from this point forward. Anything less than total surrender is unacceptable. If you comply, then I will control your life circumstances in order to guarantee your realization. But I cannot force this on you. You must choose it. What is your decision?"

I seriously doubt She said all of this. She is a Divine Mother of few words! But that is the essence of what She said to me. Without hesitation, I said "Yes. I surrender completely to you. I give my life over to you. My life is yours now."

She smiled. Then just as quickly as She had appeared, Her Presence was gone.

When I asked somebody on the grounds about the Temple being open with the statue of Kali there, he acted surprised. The next time I visited the temple Her statue had been moved behind an iron fence. Kali in jail! I laughed out loud.

In early 1988, out of the blue the thought came to me that "My last name has the name of God, Ram, in it, so my guru is going to have Ram in his name." The thought just kept repeating over and over.

At this same time, I experienced a strange but not unpleasant metallic taste in the middle of my tongue. I have not felt that taste since. My impression is it was from Akasha (the etheric element).

A few months later I saw Ramesh's picture in a Hollywood paper. I instantly knew it was him. I intuitively knew with total certainty that meeting him was my destiny. He was going to change my life.

So what did I do? I decided to wait a year because I wanted to have one last year before I ran into the spiritual freight train called Ramesh! Looking back at it, it was a bizarre reaction. My thought at the time was "I'm not quite ready."

Fast forward to my encounter with Ramesh Balsekar in Solana Beach, October, 1989. I saw him later at several group meetings. This first time was at "Joe's Crab Shack" with about 50 people.

I have never loved a man like I loved him. I felt that he was my spiritual father. I love my biological father totally, yet the spiritual connection with Ramesh transcended everything. The feeling was like an ocean of love. I would cry and cry tears of joy.

The last event I went to took place in Pennsylvania, USA. I finally had a chance to talk to him one on one in a way. He was hanging out after giving a talk to the large group.

When I walked rather timidly up to the small group that had gathered around him in the back of the room, he abruptly stopped talking to them and turned to me. I still remember his penetrating gaze locking my eyes in place. There was no escape from those magnificent eyes!

I said something about how much I loved him and how I wanted to come to India to be his servant. He looked genuinely shocked.

"Oh, no," he said, "that is nonsense! You should not be lingering around. I have given you everything I can give you. Go study with other teachers if you like. Or just do whatever you want. It won't matter. I have given you everything. Now you must move on with your life. I cannot help you anymore."

I said "Thank you" and reached out to give him a hug, which he accepted. The joy and gratitude you feel with the person who has revealed the Self to you simply cannot be described. So even though this was the last thing I wanted to hear, I intuitively knew he was right. I never saw him again. He lives on in my heart and in my life.

My journey then took me back to Sri Nisargadatta Maharaj and Sri Ramana Maharshi. I studied their teachings all over again and practiced the unique meditations they taught.

In 2006, the Kundalini completed Her journey to the Crown chakra. A secret passageway from the Crown down to the Heart on the right called Amrita Nadi was revealed to me.

There was a life-transforming flash of Amrita Nadi. It was the ultimate spiritual event of my life. Amrita Nadi ("channel of immortality") and Hridayam (the causal Heart on the right side of the chest) are mainly talked about by Sri Ramana Maharshi.

The awakening of Amrita Nadi has been described as "the light of a thousand suns." The world turns translucent and disappears in a blaze of Divine Light. When the world returns, it is not the same world. That world is gone forever. There is only the one supreme Self. You can still perceive the world and function in the world, but for you the world is literally the universal Self.

As I write this, I am reminded of the spontaneous Kundalini event of 1966. I have come full circle. The Light that was revealed in 1966 was the Light that was realized in 2006.

Sri Ramana Maharshi on Self-Inquiry, the I-Thought and the Heart on the Right

As all living beings desire to be happy always, without misery, as in the case of everyone there is observed supreme love for one's self, and as happiness alone is the cause for love, in order to gain that happiness which is one's nature and which is experienced in the state of deep sleep where there is no mind, one should know one's self. For that, the path of knowledge, the inquiry of the form "Who am I?", is the principal means.

What is called mind is a wondrous power existing in Self. It projects all thoughts. If we set aside all thoughts and see, there will be no such thing as mind remaining separate; therefore, thought itself is the form of the mind. Other than thoughts, there is no such thing as the world.

Sri Ramana Maharshi

Knowledge itself is "I." The nature of (this) knowledge is existence-consciousness-bliss. Of all the thoughts that rise in the mind, the thought "I" is the first thought."

That which rises in this body as "I" is the mind. If one inquires "In which place in the body does the thought 'I' rise first?," it will be known to be in the heart [the spiritual heart which Ramana says is "two digits to the right from the center of the chest"]. Even if one incessantly thinks "I", "I", it will lead to that place (Self).

The mind will subside only by means of the inquiry "Who am I?"

The thought "Who am I?", destroying all other thoughts, will itself finally be destroyed like the stick used for stirring the funeral pyre.

If other thoughts rise, one should, without attempting to complete them, inquire, "To whom did they arise?", it will be known "To me." If one then inquires "Who am I?," the mind (power of attention) will turn back to its source. By repeatedly practicing thus, the power of the mind to abide in its source increases. (2)

How to Do Self-Inquiry Meditation

In a few words, the goal is to drop the mind into the Heart. The mind thrives on complication. Here is a simple summary to help you. This method of Self-inquiry is direct, powerful and effective.

(A) PEACE, HAPPINESS, LOVE & JOY = THE HEART (on the Right).

From the HEART the I-thought ("I am the body" idea) RISES swiftly up to the HEAD.

The I-thought is now WANDERING free. This produces endless possibilities for interaction with apparent "other" people, places, things, situations and endless opportunities for endless confusing problems.

The outcome is the Conventional Experience of the so-called WORLD. This illusory "world" is suffering, conflict, doom and gloom... sort of like the movie "The Matrix."

(B) The SOLUTION is to deliberately REVERSE this sequence of events where the mental Head takes over and the Heart of pure feeling is abandoned and forgotten....

Lost in many THOUGHTS about world and other people (UP in the HEAD)....

You TRACE any given complex thought back to the isolated SOLO I-THOUGHT....

CONSCIOUS of the path of the solo I-thought back down to the Heart (on the right)....

You boldly and assertively CHALLENGE the arrogant deceitful ROGUE I-thought....

(1) "WHO ARE YOU?" or "WHO IS HAVING THIS THOUGHT?

To which the I-thought replies, "I am."

(2) "WHERE DID YOU COME FROM?"

To which the I-thought replies, "From the Heart."

"CRESTFALLEN" (Ramana's words), the I-thought falls back DOWN into the HEART.

(C) Back HOME, You REST in the HEART = PEACE, HAPPINESS, LOVE & JOY

(D) REPEAT as Often as Needed ...Until It Is No Longer Needed... and You Are FREE.

Note: To help with identifying and diving into the I-thought, repeating "I-I" is also effective. The final flower of the path of Self-inquiry meditation is abiding in the thought-free state. This is not different from resting in the pure unbounded Feeling of Being.

A book on Self-inquiry that was quite helpful to me and I highly recommend is "The Path of Sri Ramana, Part One" by Sri Sadhu Om. In Chapter Eight, Sri Sadhu Om gives the quintessence of Self-inquiry. He states "Therefore, all that we are to practice is to be still with the remembrance of the feeling I." This remarkable book is currently free as a PDF download from the web site of Michael James, the esteemed translator. (3)

This "feeling I" that Sri Sadhu Om is referring to is the First Person "I." He plainly states that the teaching of Sri Ramana Maharshi is to find the True I, the Self, you must dwell in the feeling of being the "first person." When you find your attention being diverted to the second or third person, return your attention to the first person.

The first person is "I." The second person is "you." The third person is "them." So if I am talking to you about her or about him or about it, then we have included all three steps away from the Self. We are now fully engaged in the so-called "world."

Sri Sadhu Om Swamigal

When you think about it, that covers everything in the world. No matter what it is, it is either about me, about you or about them! So simple, yet it is true.

To help you return to the pure "I" FEELING OF BEING of the first person "I," you can ask yourself "To whom do these thoughts appear?" or "Who is thinking these thoughts?" These more concrete variations of "Who am I?" make more sense to some people.

So Self-inquiry is "Abiding in the Self" by staying with and, as much as possible, staying silently in the pure state of feeling-being that is the natural "first person" I. Sri Sadhu Om enthusiastically says "Sadhana is not doing, but being!"

What dawns eventually is the realization that the feeling of "I" that we naturally have is not wrong at all. It is right on target. The mistake is to think that it is the signifier of the first person who is then defined in terms of relationships to second and third persons.

All of this is based on the seductive nonsense of the widespread experience, which is really a sort of hypnosis, that "I am the body." This experience is just an experience of an idea, of a belief. It is a kind of mind control on this planet. It is a global trance.

Just as people at one time were convinced that the world was flat and lived their lives accordingly, most people believe "I am the body" and live accordingly. But when the truth is seen, that they are the pure unfettered "I," the unlimited True I that is the Self, then everything changes in an instant. Truth is Truth, and it will set you free.

The Two Stages of Self-Inquiry

The path of Self-inquiry has two stages. The first stage is to greatly reduce the number of thoughts you are having each day. The second stage is to dive deep into the Heart, into this quiet mind, in order to confront, uproot and dissolve the ring leader I-thought.

Passive witness "just watching" meditation is enough to fulfill the first stage, but it is not enough to expose the I-thought ("I am the body" idea). It still lurks below the surface. You may enjoy a quiet mind, but you have not realized the pristine natural state.

To fulfill your spiritual potential and complete the second stage, you must now switch gears and be aggressive. During meditation, you will need to notice, confront and knock down EVERY single thought that rises up.

There are two good reasons to do this. The first is that even if just a few thoughts are allowed to go by unnoticed and gather together, that will be sufficient to create the illusion of others and the world.

The second reason is even more critical. As long as you allow these secondary thoughts to rise up unchallenged, the leader of the thought gang, the I-thought, will not come out of hiding. He will feel safe and secure. He knows that he is still in charge.

While noticing, confronting and knocking down each and every thought may seem impossible while you are active in the world, you must still strive for it. During meditation, you must make your top effort to be aware of and pounce on every single thought.

Each thought that arises is about the I-thought. Each thought that arises is an expression of the I-thought. Your thoughts are "about me" and that "me" is the I-thought, not the unbounded true Self. This "me" refers to the physical body.

As you transition to the second stage, there will still be a tendency to "watch the watcher." The one that is watching the watcher is just another thought. It is the pseudo-self, the thinker-experiencer.

You want pure awareness to come forward. Awareness pounces on the arising thought. It eats it and dissolves it. There is left just the experience itself. No thinker is left. No experiencer echo remains.

In the beginning, it may seem like the thoughts are endless. If you persist, this will change. Then you reach the fulfillment of the first stage, the quiet mind. Just watching thoughts will get you this far.

When you make the required effort in the second stage, it may seem once again that the work is endless and nearly fruitless. If you persist, the thought-free true Self or natural state will begin asserting itself. A serene untouched pristine state comes forward.

This natural state appear to be like the thought-free state of the quiet mind, but it is beyond it. It is the primal state. It is the original state. It is actually a "stateless state," truly transcendental.

It has never been polluted by thought. It has always been thought free. It comes forward bigger and stronger. It abides longer and longer. Eventually, you realize that this pure beautiful magnificent Beingness without stain or blemish is the real you.

Finally, your true Self asserts its dominance. The full power of its pure unadulterated Presence embraces, dissolves and destroys the I-thought. It returns to the Heart and dies there. What remains is your true Self, the natural state of Peace, Love and Happiness.

The foundation for this realization is the thought-free state. This state is NOT easily achieved. Do not be fooled. It is difficult!

This Self-inquiry sadhana requires that you (a) be aware of EVERY single thought that arises moment to moment and (b) that you do something in awareness that interrupts that thought's tendency to go out into the world, connect with other thoughts and so on.

This is non-negotiable. The goal is to be able to abide in the thought-free state for long periods of time, for several minutes at least.

This is samadhi. It is fine if you can only achieve the thought-free state under the ideal conditions of deep sitting meditation. Nobody expects you to be able to abide in the thought-free state out in the world while being busy unless you've attained enlightenment.

Your enlightened natural state is literally without thoughts. Thoughts may come and go within it, but it makes no difference to you.

Your body can wear a red shirt now and a minute later a blue shirt. That does not make your body first red and then blue. The coming and going of thoughts makes no difference to the natural state.

But in order to arrive at that natural state and be established in it, you must first be able to abide in the thought-free state for more than a few seconds. Being able to repeatedly reach and consistently stay for at least a few minutes in the pure thought-free state during sitting meditation is a good start. It may even be enough to achieve the spiritual breakthrough. But that would be the bare minimum.

The I-Feeling Is More Than Just a Feeling!

The mind cleverly maintains a fog of complexity and confusion. The message of Ramana attacks this fog directly by reducing the vast drama of the mind down to one thought, the I-thought. This I-thought can be known first-hand, experienced and overcome.

The challenge of overcoming the mind becomes simply the challenge of discerning the I-thought and studying its true nature. You separate it out from the rest of the thoughts. The root of the mind is the I-thought. The beginning and the end of the mind is the I-thought.

To get rid of the mind and the problems it produces, pull it out by the root. This means identify, separate out and destroy the I-thought by returning it to the Heart of pure unconditioned feeling. This is experienced in meditation as the thought-free state.

When the mind, meaning the I-thought, is destroyed, then there is the unbroken Peace that surpasses understanding. It is not a special state. It is your natural state.

In fact, it is not really a "state" at all. When you remember who you are, then all of this becomes obvious. It is the way it is. It was never any other way. You are you and that is that. In the words of Advaita Vedanta, I AM THAT.

You promised to make this simple. Can you make it any simpler? How about three things to remember?

Okay, but I have to give you four keys. The fourth is really a repeat of the third, but in a different form. At least that's true once you understand it.

The First Key: You are the I-feeling.

Just think about it. Where would you be without the I-feeling? The body is just a machine.

The Second Key: You are not the body.

By that I mean you are not the dream body or astral body either. I will get into that.

The Third Key: Self-realization (enlightenment) is bringing the deep sleep state into the waking state.

We enter into the deep sleep state every night, so we do have access. The trick is in making it conscious.

The Fourth Key: You Are That right now (the Sun of the Heart is shining bright behind the clouds).

Number four comes from number three automatically because you are already accessing the deep sleep state. It's a part of your experience every night. In this sense, you have the Self, you are the Self, but you have not realized it.

You are accessing the Self in deep sleep every night, only it is not conscious. Advaita is to make it conscious.

I have the experience that I am the I-feeling in a body. Mostly I feel that I am behind my eyes. The I-feeling feels like a little place in the center of my head. It's not always like that, but that's probably the most common place.

Good, that is very precise. As far as I know, that's a common experience. There are plenty of variations, but "the I behind the eyes" seems to be the most widespread experience of the limited body-confined I-feeling.

She just said she is the I-feeling, only stuck in her body, so how is your first point "You are the I-feeling" any different than what she is talking about?

What I mean is that you are exclusively the I-feeling. You are the I-feeling and nothing else. When you experience the true unbounded I-feeling in all of its glory and totality, then there is nothing else. There is only this one supreme "I."

That sounds mystical, but it is exactly this same small I-feeling that seems to be stuck in the prison cell of the physical body. The I-feeling stuck in the body is the limited ego experience. The I-feeling free of body identification is infinite.

So that would be the message of the second pointer, to drop the body?

Yes, exactly. The formula for our suffering is I-Feeling Plus "I am the body" Thought Equals Life-Long Suffering. The solution is found by subtracting the "I am the body" thought from the equation. You are left with I-feeling only. As the pure unbounded I-feeling, there is simple the indescribable joy of the feeling of being free without limits. You know that, at long last, you are now truly you. You have arrived home.

The soaring of an eagle is symbolic of that. The thrill of beautiful inspiring music is a taste of that. I am free, free, free... free at all places... free at all times... free. Not just free to be this or that. Not just free to become someone or something. Free right here as whatever arises. Free here and now. Everything rises and falls within this freedom, inside this wide open fullness.

This freedom is beyond wild craziness and rule-bound sanity. Shinzen Young, a brilliant Buddhist meditation teacher who was so helpful to me in my first years as a serious dedicated student of the Self, called it being "super-sane." You function just fine in this world. You are super-sane, in the world and a master of it, but not of it. You can touch it, but it cannot touch you. You have transcended the world. You have overcome the world. You are the world. There is no more world.

But what about all of the thoughts, thousands of thoughts each day? I don't go around saying to myself "I am the body, I am the body." Instead I'm thinking about what to make for dinner, are the kids okay, when is my husband getting home, will he have to work late again?

The identification takes place early. For me, it happened when I was about two and a half years old. That was when I accepted the programming, the cultural hypnosis that I am this body with this name.

I was joyfully jumping up and down in my crib. My parents kept saying my first name over and over. All of a sudden, there was a snap in my head. Everything came into sharp focus and I "knew" that I was this body and name.

Up to that point, I had just been play acting, just going along with my big benefactors. But now I was stuck. I felt the confinement immediately. I had taken on a huge burden but there was nothing I could do about it at the time.

I think it makes sense that the identification with the body takes place very young. We start living as if we are the body even before we go to kindergarten. But where does all the thinking come from?

Life does not like raw duality, the unresolved only two. It creates a triangle from the I-feeling and the "I am the body" thought. Three becomes the new stable unity. When there's just two, it is a stand-off. The third point of the triangle is the world-involvement of the I-thought. This is the outgoing thinking each day that typically is about your relationships with other people and the daily news.

To be technically correct, the "I am the body" thought IS the I-thought, but as you said, you spin off into secondary thoughts all day long. What develops from that next is your story. So now you are the body with a certain name who is in the world and now has a story. Based on this back story, you have your thoughts that never want to stop.

If you examine your thoughts closely, you will see they are about only three categories.

There is you as the first person. There are others in the form of people, animals and things that you personally know. They are the second person. Then there are people, animals and things in the world that you don't personally know. They are the third person.

For example, when you hear about a celebrity in the news, that is third person. Your entire experience of the world can be broken down into first person, second person and third person.

That's an interesting analysis. I never thought of those categories. Even so, it's a gigantic mess. There's a world with seven billion people. How can we ever get out of it?

The answer is you could not unless it was already the case that you are free of it. The reason for the third key, the third main point where I am making my effort to make Advaita as simple as I can, is that the truth lives in your deep sleep state. The Silence is already there. It is there 24 hours a day. It is there during the day as well as the night.

Because you already are that Silence, that Wholeness, that Brightness, then you can remember it and be what you already are. If you had to create it by fighting your body and mind, the battle would be hopeless. You cannot invent or manufacture happiness. If you were not already happy and free, then happiness and freedom would be impossible.

But getting to the deep sleep state sounds like a difficult task.

I said it was simple, I didn't say it was easy! It is straightforward, provided you remember what you're doing. The second key is that you are not the body. Well, that includes the dream body, too. It is no big deal for us to dream and have a dream body in our dreams.

It is amazing, but that dream body that is the action body for the dream state while we are in the dream state feels every bit as real as this physical body that is the action body for the waking state. When you think about it, that's pretty bizarre. That's like saying we have two bodies — a day action body and a night action body.

Sounds pretty schizophrenic, yet everybody seems just fine with that. Even your down home beer drinking truck driving country cousin — if you have one — is okay with it! Even so, right there is a big hint for those of us who are investigating this.

There is an error that people then tend to make which is that they think this dream body is just a creative fantasy based on being the physical body. But the dream body is far more than that. The dream body can change shapes, even have a different sex or be an animal or be some mythical creature. This dream body is also called the astral body.

The main thing that the dream state body and the waking state body have in common is the feeling of embodiment. They both have this basis in the idea of "I am the body." In the physical body, we think it is limited to just this one body. In the dream body, we are set free to be many things, but we are still just a body, limited to a body of some kind.

So that raises the question "If what dream and waking have in common is bodyness, then where does this common idea of being a body come from?" If there is a period during sleep when we are not the body, that is where we need to look.

The answer to where the body idea comes from is the silent deep sleep state. It is only in the deep sleep state that we lose all awareness of being the body. For this reason, it is deeply regenerating. In the deep sleep state are hidden all of the core ideas, the archctypes, the great patterns out of which the dream worlds and the physical worlds are manifested.

When you look closely at them, you see that both the physical and dream worlds are synthetic. They are expanding upon and synthesizing from great ideas, but where did these amazing ideas, these patterns, these templates come from? They came from the universal causal dimension. Our personal access to that is called our deep sleep state.

So when you trace the I-feeling plainly like this, it is immediately exposed that the real switch is not from physical to dreaming, but from feeling of "I am the body" to the feeling of being bodiless and back again. So the significant cycle is not from physical to dreaming and back again, as people believe.

The important cycle is from embodiment or a body identified state to being without a body, to a formless state. The causal dimension or deep sleep state is experienced as formless, but it contains the seeds of form in it. Even if you call it a "causal body," the experience is formlessness.

In the causal state, it is a pleasant refreshing nothingness. It is a featureless Silence. It is the deep rest of absolutely nothing going on. It is little eery, like the silence of the dead in a graveyard. There is something alive about it yet something is strange about it. It is like being with somebody who is in a coma. So they are here and they are not here. But all the potential for manifestation, for involvement in the dream and waking worlds, is resting in there ready to go.

The causal body is like a big dark treasure room. When I say it is dark, it is pitch black. It seems there is nothing of value in it. When you turn the light on, the darkness goes away instantly. Now you can see all the amazing treasures, including the master templates for everything that manifests down the line in the dream worlds and physical worlds.

When the light is turned on for good, that is realizing the Self. It is your room and you had already visited it many times in deep sleep while you were unconscious. But before it was always pitch black dark and you just fell asleep when you got there. It did not dawn on you that something incredibly valuable could be hidden in the deep black darkness.

This is intentional. For whatever reason, part of the cosmic plan is to make it difficult to arrive at this understanding. The secrets are hidden in plain sight since we visit the causal storehouse every night, but they are cloaked in darkness and unconsciousness, so this is not easily seen. Unless somebody tells you about it, you might never realize this.

When you say we are bringing the deep sleep state into the waking state, I guess it makes sense if the deep sleep state is silent, but how do we do that? It seems to me the only time I access the deep sleep state is when I'm sleeping, not even sleeping, but sleeping deeply, and then I don't remember anything other than maybe I slept well.

Yes, that's the problem, isn't it? It is helpful to know that the deep sleep state is already Silent and without thoughts, so maybe we can just embrace it and be done with it. But how do we do that? Any ideas?

I guess by being quiet in the waking state. We have to challenge the I-thought as it rises up.

Yes, that is correct. The truth is that for most people, it is hard work. I worked at it for many years. I will not lie. It was difficult. If I had had the help of Ramana's teachings early on, who knows?

But the truth is, I was exposed to his teachings years ago. To be honest, I did not understand what he was saying. The notion of doing a scientific technique, tested and proven, made more sense. So I was into Buddhist Vipassana body-sweeping meditation for years and years. Insight meditation is based on studying change which is very scientific. I related to a method where you put in your time and effort and you could expect to be paid back in spiritual progress.

The short super-concentrated answer as you said is that you challenge the rising of the I-thought at every turn. Your goal is to challenge it each time it shows up, each time it rises up. Then you return to rest in the Silence. There will be a gap of peaceful silence right after you challenge the I-thought. Then the thought noise will start up again.

At some point, you begin to realize, you start to see it and feel it and know it for yourself, that this pure Silence, this deep Silence that is ever thought-free, always without thought, totally different from and prior to thought, is YOU! Then it becomes much easier. Then you know you are just returning to what you already are. Your doubts dissolve.

The process can be described like this: Recognize, Remember, Rest and Realize. So first you Recognize that you are the Silence or the Self. You get that at some real level.

Then you make the sustained effort day by day to Remember it. Eventually, as the Silence gets stronger and deeper and more natural, then you are able to Rest in it easily and naturally.

Finally, you shift into the deep let-go of total relief, the sweet timeless serenity, the amazing paradoxical fullness of Realization. Paradoxical because you were doing less and less and feeling more and more fulfilled on your way here. Now that you're actually here, you've stopped completely. Now you have everything yet you are doing nothing. Now you're abiding in Realization.

Even then you may go back and forth between Resting and Realizing until you are completely stabilized in it. Once you are fully established in Realizing, you will know it. Your questions will end. No more questions. No conflicts. No dilemmas. No problems. No confusion. No doubts. Your doubts will be gone. You are free and you know it.

When you are stabilized in it, then it won't matter where you are or what you are doing. The world goes away. There is only the Self

The world is just thoughts, thoughts layered upon thoughts. The Self is ever without thoughts. When the Self is, the world is not.

For this reason, the world takes on a transparent or translucent quality. All the color and details are there, but not the sense of reality. It looks like a dynamic interactive hologram to you. It is just a projection of the Self, a creative expression of the Self. It is a brilliant amazing construct, yet because it is just a construct, it is nothing.

So when you stabilize in the Self, you can still see the world and function in the world, but the world is not real to you. It is not real to you because you know it is just a thought. A thought can be described and experienced, but it cannot be called real. It is not real to you also because you know it is you. It literally is you. Everything is you. Actually, it is not quite correct to call it a thought. There is only the Self. Though it can be experienced, there is no world at all.

The functioning of the Self is automatic and without thoughts. It may seem that thoughts are used, or that words are being used, just as here when I am talking. But I don't have the experience that I am talking. My experience is that I am just being. Nothing is happening. It is like the TV over there is talking. Just like you, I don't know what the TV is going to say next. Like you, I am listening to hear what the TV is going to say. I don't know any more than you do.

My experience is that there is only the Self, only this one ultimate authentic genuine unbounded pure "I." Furthermore, I know that You Are That. I know that you are the Self, that there is nothing other than the Self, so at times I must be reminded that there is supposed to be somebody else talking or that somebody else is supposed to exist who is supposed to be having these problems.

There are no problems in my universe. There is only the Self, and because the Self has no thoughts in it, it has no problems. Thought is the beginning of problems. The end of thought is the end of problems.

I know there is nobody else, but since the apparent "other people" seem to think they exist separate from me and from each other , then I must address them where they are in their beliefs in order to communicate with them. Frankly, it is total nonsense to me, but that is life. I know you really are the Self.

I know that eventually you will come around, so I am okay with this process. Maybe you got knocked hard on your head and you forgot who you are. Soon you will wake up and remember. So just like that, I believe you could wake up in the next minute or this afternoon or tomorrow.

What Is Advaita or Non-Duality?

The spiritual journey is paradoxical. There is a path and there is no path. Yet when you think about it, everyday life is just the same.

You get up in the morning and eat your breakfast. Where did the breakfast come from? How did it go from being eggs to being an omelet? After you eat it, where does it go?

All day long we are walking the pathless path and thinking it is "the world." Everything is a magic act. Everything is disappearing. As soon at it appears, it disappears.

Your body today is not the same body it was yesterday. Nothing is as it seems. In reality, there is only the Self, only universal consciousness, only natural pure awareness. There is no world as such. There is only the Self. It is our Christ Nature or our Buddha Nature.

This Self includes in it the potential for experiencing the so-called "world," but this world is not and never was independent and free-standing. The world is an "ornament" of the Self.

The "world" is like an ephemeral dream. It is like a Hollywood movie. It is all appearance. It is all show. It is smoke and mirrors. It is the magic act of a gifted master magician. There is no substance. Nonetheless, it can still be experienced.

It is you that give it reality and meaning, not the other way around. Because you are, everything is. With or without all of that other stuff, you are forever you. You give birth to the universe. The universe is inside of you. You are the Source. You are the Ultimate.

What is Advaita or non-duality?

The best answer to that is probably silence, the thought-free state. The reality is that there is only the Self. The Self is everything. Everything is the Self.

So anything called "advaita" or "non-duality" is just a concept. It is just words. Since it is just words, you look it up in a dictionary or an encyclopedia. You look it up online.

Yes, but it's a great spiritual tradition.

Of course it's a great spiritual tradition. Sri Ramana Maharshi was and is the crowning jewel of that tradition. Before him Sri Shankara and King Janaka. But non-duality is pretty much the holistic religious message of India. So you can have qualified non-duality and so on when somebody is very devotional, very bhakti. Maybe Sri Ramakrishna would go under that category. But the names are just on the surface. It's all different flavors of non-duality.

Then you've got Yogananda. He was in the Kundalini yoga tradition and he got Self-realized. It goes on and on. The point is not that the Advaita of Ramana is the only way or the right way or the true way or any of that. The point is that you as an individual human being must find your own way. You must listen to your heart and follow it. There is no one path for everybody. There is one right path for you, and if you care enough about spirituality to pursue it with full dedication, with the willingness to make the necessary sacrifices, then that path will be made straight and clear for you.

But the main problem on this planet is that people simply don't care. That may be changing, the vibration may be lifting, but the disease of the ages has been that people just don't care! An individual here or there cares, but the mass, the vast majority of the people, really are like sheep. They go wherever their masters lead them. They are obsessed with clothing the body, with status, with money, with entertainment, with celebrities.

It is beyond absurd. It is so ridiculous I can hardly talk about it. The people can blame no one but themselves. They don't care about God. Going to church once or twice a week is not caring about God. That's maintaining an insurance policy. Loving God means you love God more than you love your own life. Loving God means you WANT to die for God. You look forward to it, to your total final death in God.

I have given up on talking to these people. It is like talking to a brick wall. Everybody honestly truly believes that they are right, that they are seeing things clearly. The world that they see is the real world. They have no doubt of that. This is incredibly amazing because they are 100 per cent wrong! They are suffering yet their minds are closed shut.

I see plenty of evidence of spirituality.

Yes, there's trace elements of it. But the dominant themes are collecting stuff for the body, being entertained, making more and more money. It is all about "I am the body."

Many more people are now doing yoga and meditating.

I'll never forget the first TV commercial I saw where it showed some hot girls in Hollywood doing yoga. It was a classic infomercial. Maybe you've seen it. What they were selling — I am not making this up — what they were selling was a DVD on how to get a "yoga butt." A yoga butt? Are you kidding me?

These women are doing yoga and all they care about is getting a "yoga butt." Six thousand years of yoga, of the supreme science, and now, finally, at long last, the crowning achievement of hatha yoga is these Hollywood bimbos building up their "yoga butts." Of course, there are many serious yogis like you are saying.

Wow. I never saw that commercial.

It's a classic. At first I was in a state of shock. I couldn't believe my eyes. In all seriousness, I thought maybe it was a comedy spoof of some kind. I said something to my wife and she said "Oh yeah, don't you know about that? Getting a yoga butt is the latest thing. Everybody wants that tight yoga bubble butt."

She looked at the video. "Oh yeah, those bitches are hot!" She pointed to one of the girls on screen. "See, look at her butt. Now that is one hot butt!" Then she went back to what she was doing. It was no big deal for her. Of course you want a yoga butt. Yoga butts are hot!

Well, if you wanted proof that this world is completely crazy, that yoga butt commercial is all you need. That is my point exactly. People think all of this is totally real, normal, sensible. They don't investigate. They aren't even curious. They take it at face value and don't go any deeper. Hey, having a good yoga butt is all that matters.

I think you're making too much out of this infomercial. Why make such a big deal? It is kind of funny.

You asked me what Advaita or non-duality is. That is how we got here. What I'm pointing out is what it is not. Yes, it's funny but why is it funny? It's funny because it shows us how as a culture we are missing the mark.

Advaita or non-duality is not yoga butts. So if you are stuck at the yoga butt level, you've got a long ways to go. Not if you *have* a yoga butt — just if you're *stuck* there! In Zen, they have a saying: "Not one, not two." I think that is a really cool saying because in four words they address the main problem with thinking about Advaita as a concept.

The word "non-duality" is like saying "not two." But when you go "not two" your mind, because it thinks in terms of opposites, it instantly creates the concept of "one." So when you talk about or think about "not two," then your mind automatically puts up this concept of "one." If it's not two, then it must be one. But the Zen masters are on top of that. They say "Nope, it's not one, either. Sorry!" They are absolutely right.

The Sanskrit word "advaita" also means "not two." "Dvaita" which I believe is properly pronounced "dwight-uh" with a "w" means two or split in two. But the "a" at the front negates it. So Advaita then literally means "not two." The "two" in English becomes the notion of "duality." Add the "non" in front of it and you have the English version for the Sanskrit word. Non-duality.

So are you teaching Advaita or non-duality?

No, not really. I am not teaching those things. I love and honor the traditions, but it would not be correct to say I am teaching those things. I am teaching from my own experience. I discovered the Heart and Amrita Nadi in my journey to the Self. I have checked my experience against the reports of those who have gone before me, and my experience checks out. I am teaching about the Self.

One of the reasons I ended up focusing on the words and teachings of Ramana Maharshi is that he is the only one I could find who talked about the Heart and Amrita Nadi. Later I learned about Sri Lakshmana Swamy and the late American guru A. Ramana, but Ramana remains the greatest authority.

So my experience, while it did not need a validation, is still validated by the Advaita tradition. That said, there's nothing to say. The moment you open your mouth you're telling lies. So then I could talk about the Self and say "Everything is the Self. The World has no reality apart from the Self. The Self is All. There is only the Self." That is all true.

But if that is all that I say, unless a person has, so to speak, "tasted" the Self, then they don't know what I am talking about. So that's how we end up in discussions like this one talking about yoga butts! Actually, yoga butts are just as non-dual as anything else. We have come full circle. Since the world is the Self, a beautiful yoga butt is the Self, too!

I remember when somebody got mad at you for saying money is the Self. Now yoga butts are the Self. You are just digging yourself deeper and deeper into the muck, aren't you? Digging the proverbial hole! Good luck with that.

You are so right! Yes, we must start a yoga butt religion right away and make millions. Talk about a business with a great bottom line! Okay, now I've gone too far.

Well, I've got nothing to lose now. The point is that everything is the Self, literally everything. There is no person, place or thing that is not the Self. The phenomenon we call the world totally depends on the Self. The Self is what gives it whatever degree of reality it seems to have. But the realness of it is the Self, not the world.

The entire universe is inside the Self. The Self stands free and clear from all of that, from all phenomena. It is not touched by anything that is changing. If it was, then the Self would just be another changing part. There would have to be some other unchanging perfect reality that functions as the absolutely stable foundation for all of this.

The "I Am the Body" Idea: From Incarnation to Incarceration

The rising of the I-thought up to the brain from the Heart on the right is not a metaphor. It rises up or shoots up and takes over the brain. From there, it takes over the body. Then it is able to produce the terrifying noir delusion of a grim, dark and desperate world.

The original and ultimate mind control master is the I-thought. The mind arises with it. When it disappears and is gone for good, the mind goes with it. The mind is really just a bunch of thoughts. These thoughts appear as needed and then go away.

The only reason that there appears to be a coordinating center to the mind is the persistence of the apparently separate pseudo-self, the I-thought. This I-thought has falsely identified itself with the physical body and claimed the body as its own.

When the I-thought dissolves, then the so-called "mind" is experienced as pure unconditioned awareness. This natural pure awareness is like the wide open blue sky.

If thoughts appear, they are like clouds drifting through. They are natural. They are not a problem. Even though they appear to be different from the sky, they are one with the sky.

Likewise, there is no world. The world is just a thought, a concept, a cloud in the sky. No mind and no world means peace here and now. The human heart intuits this refreshing spring of sweet pure peace and yearns for it. In the Heart, the secret of silence is found.

You are always coming back to the "I am the body" idea. But I don't know why. I don't really know what that means. Why is it so important?

I get that exact phrase from Sri Ramana Maharshi. He would say it often. He said it is the root of the ego. The "I am the body" idea is the root of the false separate "doing" self.

Doership is also called "agency." The investigation of agency is pretty much a foreign concept in the West except for the philosophers. We are dedicated to taking action.

That is the common advice: you are thinking too much, take action, make things happen. You get that in sales a lot. It's just a numbers game. Make more calls and you will get more sales. In our American society, there's nothing worse than being a passive lazy street person lying on the sidewalk. Sometimes I think Americans get more irked by lazy bum homeless people than they do by gun toting killers who go postal. Hey, at least that guy who killed 20 people at the school or the church or the post office was taking action! At least he did something!

Of course, that kind of reaction points to the madness behind it all. Look at the military-industrial war complex. They have to keep starting new wars to make new profits. That boils down to killing people for money, making X dollars per head. Insane! But I digress... My reason for emphasizing that concept, besides the fact that Maharshi repeated it so often, is that it cuts through the non-duality intellectual mumbo jumbo that I hear so much nowadays. You know "The freedom of the now is the awareness of being present in the space of objective timeless non-conceptual clarity."

There is no need for a new fancy specialized vocabulary. There is no need for complex word games and mind puzzles. The whole problem is that you think that you are the physical body. The reality is that you are NOT the physical body at all. It is so simple, almost too simple. No need to read Advaita books or take classes. Are you really your body or not?

Ramana says get rid of the idea that you are the physical body and you're good. You're home free. Doing that will knock out the idea that you are the astral body or the mental body or the causal body, all of that. That is what he said. So you can be comfortable with doing the work in the conscious waking state. Just work right here. You don't have to learn lucid dreaming or try to figure out how to stay conscious in the state of deep sleep in the middle of the night.

So I like to hammer away at that core insight. For those familiar with new age or occult concepts, then they may think I am saying that then you are your astral body or your soul body or your star body or your future self body or your causal body. But what I am saying is that you are "no body" at all. In reality, you just plain do NOT have a body. Awareness does not have a body. It is present but it has no body, no location. It is everywhere. It is everything.

I don't know what to do with that. It seems to me if I am not my body, then I am dead.

Have you heard of "neti neti," meaning "not this and not that"? Well, you can start that way because anything that you can observe, look at, study, investigate, anything that is, in essence, *outside* of you, is not you. It cannot be you.

Okay, keeping it very simple, since I can look at and feel and touch and experience this chair, I can say "I am not the chair." But you are saying I can do that with my own body.

Yes, but doing it with the chair is not scary. Doing it with your own body can be frightening if you're not ready to go there yet. In fact, I have known people who just plain could not do what you are saying.

When they went to look at their physical body, all they got was a blank or a blackness. Even though they should be able to investigate their body and discover that it is separate from them, that the reality is that they can watch and observe and witness their body, so therefore they are not the body, they did not want to see that. So they had subconsciously disabled that function.

When I close my eyes and make contact with my body, I can feel my body. But what it feels like is I am my body. My feeling of being "me" extends all the way through the body.

I'm pretty sure that is the standard experience. That is precisely why just about everybody lives life on the basis of "I am the body." A superficial exploration of "Who am I?" results in just that kind of report. So it is a fair question to ask then "What can I do?"

Exactly. What can I do? I mean I am here because I am looking for something elusive called happiness and peace of mind. To be honest, it feels artificial to be doing this thing where I'm not supposed to be my body. I don't see how that could possibly add to my happiness. What am I — a ghost?

It could be that Self-inquiry is not for you. Frankly, for many years I did a body-based practice. I did a form of Vipassana meditation that consisted of non-stop mindfulness of subtle body sensations and their changingness moment to moment. The meditation consisted of patiently and systematically scanning through the physical body to notice change and fluctuation. It was Buddhist and very logical, very scientific. At the time, that appealed to me a great deal.

So it was very physical, very kinesthetic. Since I am so "touchy feely," this worked in a very beautiful way for me. I got very good results and it changed my life. So I am convinced that we must do a practice that is a good match for our makeup. That kind of meditation is called "body sweeping" meditation. It is taught around the world by Sri Goenka and his trained teachers.

I learned it from Venerable Shinzen Young in Los Angeles. I was fortunate to learn it from him. He is a true master of meditation and alerted me to many nuances in the practice. Plus he was very supportive and encouraged me to make the meditation my own.

Well, I don't know what kind of meditation I want to do exactly. I'm just in learning mode right now. Maybe you could explain to me how this "I am the body" idea is related to happiness or to the lack of it. I don't see the connection.

Thank you, that's a great question. I like that question because that has to be what it is about in the end — how to be happy. If it is not, then why are we doing it? So let me start from the other end. What is it that reduces our happiness? Now I am going to make what sounds like an assumption. To me it is an obvious truth, but it may not seem that way to everybody here. That truth is that we are already completely happy inside, but this innate natural happiness has been covered up and suppressed.

As a baby or as a little child, you may remember at times being in a state of unreasonable extreme happiness, of ecstatic joy, for no reason at all. I certainly do. In fact, I remember being in a luminous state, being a glowing ball of light, and I was filled with bliss in this state. This was when I was a baby in my crib or crawling around on the floor.

My identification was with the glowing ball of light. The baby body was to me like a robot body. It was expected of me that I should occupy this body and learn how to use it. I did not think of it as myself. It was a machine, a tool, for me to use. I did that but I could still escape from it. So I would operate it and then float back out of it. Then came the day I got stuck in it and I could not float out of it. I remember I was stuck in the feet. Maybe because I had started walking.

As a child, you can look at a flower and be fascinated by it for hours. What is that? Well, that is child's mind. That is the mind you had before you became a serious mature functional adult. So the best of both worlds is to be a functional responsible adult and to have this pure innocent child's mind filled with wonder.

I was very happy as a child. But I haven't got a clue how to get that back. I guess that is what we are all trying to do.

Yes, the reason why we are more happy then is two-fold. First, we are not so identified with the body. We do not feel so limited by it. We have not learned to be afraid of dying. Second, we are not having very many thoughts. Everything is fresh and new. We do not have a backlog of thoughts to comment on everything and interpret everything.

I can go along with that. Definitely I have noticed that when I am more stressed out about my body, about my health, I am less happy. When my negative thoughts pile up, I am less happy. But everybody knows this stuff.

Yes, everybody who has started looking knows this stuff, but what are they doing with it? For example, you will hear that you should substitute positive thoughts for negative thoughts.

Then everything will be fine. You will attract wealth and sexy partners and drive an expensive sports car. So what? Are you really HAPPY? Or are you just entertaining yourself, eating a higher quality of junk food?

It feels better to have positive thoughts. There is no doubt that that works. If you don't fight the negative thoughts, they will drag you down. For health, too, positive thoughts are very important.

Here is my experience. Our natural state is one of unconditioned happiness. The identification with the body via the "I am the body" idea is the seed thought, the "I-thought." That one thought is the basis for all of the other thoughts, positive or negative. In our essence, we are unconditionally happy, but the thoughts come like dark clouds over the shining sun and cover our happiness. Thoughts are the culprit.

Although positive thoughts may seem like our friends, as long as they reinforce the "I am the body" thought, they are strengthening our psychological prison and constricting our happiness. Positive thoughts are an improvement but they do not take us to the Source. They do not challenge the I-thought, the secret narcissistic center of the ego process.

Thoughts tell us that they will take us to happiness, but our natural state without thoughts is the only truly happy state, the only pure state of peace, love, happiness and joy. Therefore, though positive thoughts may seem to improve our conditions, they are leading us away from true happiness. Real happiness is possible only in the unconditioned thought-free state. Thoughts are what do the conditioning. This conditioning is like hypnosis. Thoughts and words are hypnotic.

What you realize is that your love and happiness are greater when you feel less bounded by thought, less limited by thought. It is like a physical experience.

You actually feel bigger and lighter and more free, like you let go of a burden. And you did, you let go of a thought burden, of a load of thoughts.

No thought about you is true. No thought can describe you. You are the essence of happiness itself. As a baby, you are in that. As a child, you remain close to that.

Ultimately you come to the realization that the only thing that limits you is your thought. The high point of this realization about the nature of thought is that all of it starts from holding on to and embracing this "I am the body" thought. This body-identification hypnosis then gets hammered into us over and over by our parents, by our society, by everybody on the planet. Yet if you really study the situation, no thought can make you happy. Not only that, when you study the situation, you see that because people are convinced they are the body, they serve it like a slave.

This core thought that "I am the body" is like a seed that gets planted in the ground. Then the poison ivy of the ego spreads like crazy until it covers everything. In terms of the body, it spreads until the feeling of "I," the feeling of being or existing, permeates the body machine and there is the felt experience of "Yes, I really am my body!" Then the poison ivy of the ego spreads over your senses and you see and hear this troubled world. Now your trance state is complete.

This may not seem so bad, but then happiness is pursued on the basis of what brings pleasure to the body and avoiding what brings pain to the body. Yet all the while this is not for the body, it is for the mind. We can look at a corpse on a slab in a morgue. There is no mind there, no desire there, no ambition, no pain or pleasure. There is nobody there.

That's true. I used to work in a hospital. It is very disconcerting to see a corpse, especially of a young person. There is nobody home. So you understand why people think there is a soul. Something had to be animating the body.

Yes, the "soul" is the notion of an eternal "I am" that somehow has a limited or bounded form. It is a useful concept as a stepping stone to the Self, but it is important to remember that the experience of the Self is one of unboundedness. So there is something else that is driving all of this, and that something is the mind. It is the mind that goes from body to body in reincarnation. What is this mind? This mind is the I-thought. This mind is "I am this body."

Ramana Maharshi says there is one particular thought that is the seed thought that creates the whole edifice we call the mind. It is just one thought, the thought that launches this whole enterprise we call the mind, and that thought is specifically the "I am the body" thought. So the mind is able to run things because it is like a computer. The core of this computer is the thought "I am the body." It is the CPU and without it, the computer mind machine cannot work.

Because Ramana Maharshi said this, we should listen. We know he is right. So if we don't understand something he says, it is not appropriate to say he is wrong. He is not wrong. The limitation is in our understanding, not in him.

But what people also do not realize is that it does not stop there with the body. That is bad enough, but what happens next is that the world is then twisted into a dark dense shape that is completely false. The world is seen in a screwed up way through the false lens of "I am the body." When you are a little child, you don't know about any of this. A flower is a flower is a flower. It is beautiful and soft. It smells good. Its fragrance stays with you. It is like a kiss on the mind.

You do not feel the heaviness and the restriction of this stone cold prison planet coming down on you yet. That's what happens when you enter into the pre-teen and teenager stages of life. Then the world comes crashing down on you. Now you learn about war and disease and dishonesty, about betrayal and tragedy and loss. You learn about slaving away to feed the body and the other bodies that depend on your body. You learn about money, power and greed.

This big crazy world filled with suffering was thrust upon me. I did not ask for this. I seem to have inherited it. It is cold, cruel, selfish, crude, indifferent and unfair. Nobody does anything about it. It's each man for himself. You are right to call it a prison planet.

There is a progression here that starts from birth, but very few see it and understand it. When you are first incarnated — or perhaps I should say "incarcerated" — in the womb, you experience your first confinement, your first prison cell. It is dark. It is like floating or swimming very slowly in a quiet deep dark sea. It is not too bad.

For most, it is okay but for a few it gets real bad. It is fairly comfortable in there, there is an amorphous quality to it, and a numb blankness all around you, but it is okay unless your mother is taking drugs or smoking or drinking. If the mother is taking illegal drugs and so on, then it can be very difficult for the prenatal human being. If the family fights a lot the mother experiences emotional pain. This pain produces negative juices that reduce your capacities prenatally.

Then you come out of your mother and you are a baby. You don't have a sense of being differentiated from your environment yet. There is no sense of world because there is no sense of you. Notice that. If there is no you, there is no world! Due to the insistence of the parents and other people, you take on a name that society will use to label you like a can of tuna.

That becomes the assigned name for your body. Around this time, it hits you like a ton of bricks that you are your body and it has this name. I am talking about the age of two or three. As you get older, more and more you get overwhelmed by and involved in this world. But what is this world? What is it exactly?

My answer is that it is your thoughts piled up. There is no world apart from your thoughts. And what is the origin of all of these thoughts that pile up and create what seems to be the world?

The origin of all of these thoughts is the seed thought "I am the body." This idea is the hidden beginning of your suffering. Even more amazing, we walk right back into our prison every single day.

We willingly jump back into the jail cell each morning when we wake up from sleep. But if you're not interested in investigating this, I cannot help you. The motivation to do this inquiry must arise from within. If you don't care, there is not much that I can do for you.

The "I Am the Body" Idea: the I-Thought Dictator Rules the World

There is nothing wrong with the physical body. It is divine. It is perfect just as it is. This process of waking up has nothing to do with dualistic notions of there being something "wrong" or "bad" about the body or any of its functions or expressions.

When you wake up in the morning, you wake up as pure spacious luminous awareness. You wake up in a "gap" between dreaming and waking. You are that "gap," that space which is a vastness.

The I-thought, being just a thought, cannot exist without a basis, without a body. In the deep sleep state, it attaches itself to the causal body. In the dream state, it attaches itself to the astral body. In the waking state, it attaches itself to the physical body.

Most people never wonder how they are able to go from deep sleep to dream to waking. They think it is all explained by science. They believe it all happens inside the brain and that the only reality is the physical world outside of them.

This delusion is the result of the I-thought rising up very quickly in the morning and taking over your brain. It happens so fast right when you wake up that you don't notice it. It doesn't register. Then, in the words of the Bible, you see "through a lens, darkly."

You are looking at the so-called world through thick dirty dark egocentric glasses. You do not see the world as it is. In reality, the world is seamless pure Light. It is Heaven here and now. It is God. It is Love. It is the supreme Self. There is no duality. There is only One.

I want to be happy. But it seems to me that many people are very happy who still think they are the body. They enjoy the body. They celebrate the body. I don't see how a negative attitude towards the body is good.

I am not talking about having a negative attitude towards the body. The problem is not the physical body. The problem is the mind. The mind does not want to die. The mind needs a body to live. As for happy people, yes, a person can be wise and take good care of themselves. They can be loving and achieve great happiness.

What I am talking about is for people who have had enough of the so-called wheel of karma. They have been reborn as human beings hundreds of times and they are getting tired of it. When I was a teenager, I just wanted to get off this planet. I prayed that I could be taken out of here. I would cry and cry. "I don't want to be here. Take me away!"

Why do we choose to be reborn into our life prison each day when we wake up? We consent to this treatment because we are not conscious that it is happening. We are not aware of the consequences, of the price that we are paying.

I speak only from my own experience. I verify it against the teachings of great recognized sages, but if I am going to talk about it with others, I must have had the direct experience myself.

The other factor for me is that I was having a profound experience of suffering no matter what was going on. I could not shake it. I could not escape it. This began when I was a teenager. You could say I was forced to investigate it.

I have heard that before, that the reason for suffering is it makes us think of God. It will make us get serious about spirituality. But that turns God into a sadist. God's plan for us includes torturing us.

Yes. I want to explain exactly how this suffering gets installed each day. Here is what I found out. First, the "I am the body" thought appears in consciousness. Just before that, you were enjoying as pure consciousness. This happens right when you wake up from sleep. In a second or less, this seed I-thought flashes like lightning from the Heart on the right and shoots up to the Crown center and into the brain. In a second or two, it takes over the brain.

Then from the brain, also within a second or two, it spreads all through the physical body. It fills the nerves of the body with this sticky gooey false feeling of "I am the body." You could call it a nerve toxin that numbs. The boundless joy feeling of pure being gets squashed and covered over. Now the I-thought controls the body and the brain. It makes sure that this phony embodiment feeling fills up all of your body. But it doesn't stop there.

Then it expands from the confining restriction of "I am this body" into "I am this vulnerable body in a big bad overpowering world that is out there." It is like the darkness that had spread a thin film of phony superficial "I am this body" feeling now suddenly expands up into the sky and takes it over. Instead of a bright limitless horizon, there is a contraction as this darkness descends.

Instead of a bright sunny day filled with joy, there is night darkness at noon from a perpetual full eclipse of the sun. The moon covers the sun, the moon being the mind. The edges of the sun can barely be seen. The tiny portion of the sun's radiance that reaches us turns this world into a depressed shadow world. The mind has taken over. Symbolically, it is the *1984* of George Orwell.

Think special effects like in the movies. The Self is still shining free but it seems like there is this thick dark conflicted world that lives in a perpetual troubled night. It's all a trick, the smoke and mirrors of the master magician. Great magicians rely as much on their speed as anything. They also use distraction. That's what the I-thought does, too.

What is producing this eclipse of the sun? It is the moon mind of the "I am the body" idea. Who is the sun? This glorious always happy shining sun is the Self. The I-thought does not have to actually "cover the world." All it has to do is cover your seeing!

So the I-thought, being very clever and having the advantage of working undetected, monkeys with your perceptual mechanism. It expands itself in the mind, in the brain, to produce this dark distorting film that covers over your seeing and sensing capacities and confuses you.

Looking through the distorted "separation glasses" of the I-thought, you see this cold dark distant remote unfeeling "world." It is the fake world of the isolated I-thought entity. It is not the true world. You have been manipulated. You are under hypnosis. The whole world is in a "separation glasses" trance.

To quote from the Bible, from First Corinthians, Chapter 13, Verse One: "For now we see through a glass, darkly; but then face to face: now I know in part; but then shall I know even also as I am known." William Blake wrote "If the doors of perception were cleansed everything would appear to man as it is, infinite."

I am struck how the dark and desolate images of civilization in science fiction films starkly and accurately reproduce this nasty narcissistic overlay of dull darkness. The best example is perhaps the brilliant blockbuster movie "The Matrix."

If it is not the alienation of a computer-controlled future society or the scarred and scattered remnants of civilization reeling from nuclear war or artificial military plagues, it's blood-thirsty vampires or ravenous zombies or crazy clones or insane dictators or a thousand other terrifying yet plausible possibilities of how things in our world could go very very wrong.

From what I can tell, that artificial world "out there" imposed by the I-thought is for most people cold and distant and difficult. It is the cold cruel uncaring disconnected world torn asunder by the madness of wars and unbridled unrepentant greed.

It is like looking through the wrong end of a telescope. You look through it and everything is small. This is the I-thought's version. Even the stars and the moon look small. Look through the right end of a telescope and it all opens up. The universe opens up. The cosmic majesty is breathtaking.

This is interesting but it sounds very complicated! On top of that, I have not heard this stuff. It sounds very speculative. To be honest, it sounds like you are writing your own science fiction novel.

Have you heard of "Paradise Lost" by John Milton? Have you heard of the angel Lucifer? Lucifer says "I'd rather rule in hell than serve in heaven." Lucifer represents the I-thought. The I-thought doesn't care how horrible a hell he creates here on earth just as long as he doesn't have to serve God in heaven.

Just knowing this information is not going to help you much. It is when you actually see the I-thought, which is the same as the "I am the body" thought, rise up from the Heart on the right when you wake up in the morning and shoot up to the head, take over the brain and create the dark ugly world, that's when it makes a difference. That is life-changing.

Think about it. Sleeping is very strange. When we watch someone else who is sleeping, they look like they are in a coma. If they are not breathing or moving, we may worry that they are dead.

So it is pretty obvious that in that state we are not identified with the body in the same way as when we are in the conscious waking state. In order to wake up and be "the doer," to run around in the world doing stuff, we must wake up into this world and have the I-thought take the body over. The I-thought then hands us our daily menu of possibilities within its prison and we obey like sheep.

I am an action kind of person. Could you give me an example of how you would apply this in daily life?

Sure. The main thing that Self-inquiry is doing is an investigation of thoughts, a removing of the layers of thought so that we can get to this underlying dominant core thought "I am the body." This I-thought is the ring leader. He is hiding out in his headquarters. The leader of the gang is smart. He doesn't expose himself. He sends out his thugs, his organized gangs of thoughts, to gang up on you and overwhelm you. People call these painful experiences addiction, depression, possession. But it is the many overlays of thought, corded together like ropes, working in coordination.

The classic version of this inquiry or investigation is "Who am I?" But many people find that a two-step variation works better. Let's say a thought arises, a disturbing thought.

The first step is to confront this thought. You ask "Who is having this thought?" Or you could ask "To who (or whom) is this thought occurring?" Feel free to make up your own variation. The key is that you challenge the rising thought in this way. You don't assume that it is *your* thought.

What happens next is that you get an answer from that thought. It will say "Me" or "I am." This can be your big "aha" moment. This is your opportunity. It is the next step, the second step, that knocks down the I-thought.

In the second step, now that the I-thought has admitted that it is having that troublesome thought that rose up into your brain, you probe deeper. Now you ask "Who are you?" Or "Where do you come from?"

I find asking "where" works better. If you ask "who" it may spin you around in circles. There is only one place the I-thought can come from. That place is the Heart on the right or, if you prefer, the Self. You may or may not feel the Heart in relation to the body. Then embrace that it comes from the Self which is here and everywhere. The I-thought wants you to believe that you are the body. It wants you to think that all of these thoughts are yours. None of this is true.

Why does this method work?

The usual person claims all of his thoughts as his own. When he challenges the I-thought in the first step, he exposes the fact that the rising thought is not his thought, it is the I-thought's thought. Remember, it really is not your thought. You are the Self and the Self is always without thought. The Self is completely thought-free.

In the second step, you capitalize on the fact that you have just exposed the I-thought. Behind every single rising thought is the I-thought. It may not look like it is behind some thoughts, but it is behind every single thought that you have. Now you confront the exposed I-thought directly by asking him "Where do you come from? What is your origin?"

To review, first you ask "Who is having this thought?" or "To whom is this thought occurring?" The natural response will be "I am" or "To me." Then you ask "Who are you?" or "Where did you come from?" What will happen at this second step is that when you press it for an answer, it must fall back down into the pure I-feeling in the Heart.

When it answered at the first step, that was the "I am the body" thought. When it answers at the second step, you have nailed it. It cannot run to the body again. Now it has to fall back into first person I-feeling, the feeling of "I am" without the body sense. The Self is exactly that. The Self is the first person I-feeling, but pure, unrestricted and unbounded.

The Self is the exact same feeling of identity or being that you have right now minus the body identification. You do this or another meditation in order to return to the first person experience of "me" or "I am." Then you purify it of all limitations. Then the true nature of this first person "I am" feeling gets revealed.

So you don't start out asking "Who am I?" You ask the limiting thought itself "Who are you?" It is like the I-thought is invading your house. Your house is your body. You confront this invader, this thief. "Who are you? Where did you come from?"

The I-thought loves to get lost in second person and third person tangles. For example, my wife is a second person to me. If I am talking with my wife about her friend Sharon who lives 300 miles away in Phoenix, Arizona while we are at home in San Diego, then Sharon is now a "third person." She is not there with us.

I am there with my wife and my wife is there with me, but Sharon is not there. If she was there, she would be another "second person." I hope this doesn't sound too confusing. Think about it. Everybody in your world, starting with you, is first person, second person or third person. The goal of Self-inquiry is to get you to realize yourself as the first person.

This is just not making any sense. I guess I really think I am the body. Maybe some kind of physical yoga or breathing exercise or even a mantra would be better for me. I just don't get it.

When you listen, listen with your feeling. Listen with your heart, with your intuition. The "I am the body" thought is covering up your innate happiness, your natural sense of unfettered well-being. You were probably closer to it as a child. The I-thought wants to keep you thinking up in your head and keep you away from feeling with the innocent holiness of your pure heart.

The I-thought, the "I am the body" thought, rises up every morning and re-installs its dominance over your mind and body. You can catch it when it does this right at waking. When I was at that stage, I would catch it trying to sneak up to the brain. If you can catch the I-thought even once, you will see that it rises up from the Heart on the right and shoots up to the Crown. To see this is huge.

The body is the hardware. The I-thought is a virus program. The body can be run directly from the cosmic server, the Self, and then everything runs smoothly and perfectly. But the bodies on this planet are infected by the I-thought computer virus. The apparent result is a crazy mixed-up world with lots of suffering. This mad darkness is an illusion. The sun is still shining behind it.

Then it seeps down from the Crown into the brain. It spreads from the brain using neurotransmitters. It is like a dark toxic chemical goo and it extends itself all over the physical body. When this hypnotic goo spreads through the nerves of the body it creates the chemically-induced identity trance feeling "I am this body."

This false feeling is convincing. It is like taking a strong drug that disables you, numbs you out and makes you stupid. Incredibly, all of this happens in just a second or two. Like any other great illusionist, the I-thought relies on its amazing speed. If it was slow, many people would detect it. So it is lightning fast.

The "I am the body" thought has been very successful. It has hypnotized the entire world. It controls the entire world.

The I-thought, not Hitler or Stalin or some other historical figure, is the ultimate dictator. When people look out and see that the world is dark, that it is suffering, they do not realize that all of this is due to the thorough permeation of the human being with this "I am the body" idea, by this foreign thought program. It is the source and cause of suffering.

This "I am the body" thought is very good at hiding. That is why I am so grateful to Sri Ramana Maharshi for pointing it out to me. If he had not pointed it out, I don't know if I would have seen it. It is hiding underneath all of the other thoughts. So, yes, in some way you have to work through all of these covering thoughts to get to it. It is the brains behind the ingenious mind control operation that manages to blot out the beautiful ever present Light of the Self.

Since all of this is not obvious in the beginning, the process is one of elimination. We are eliminating thought patterns. Thoughts will say "I am this or that." For example, "I am a teacher, I am a gardener, I am an executive, I am a mother."

Yet when you look at these statements closely, they are possible only when you first have in place the thought, the assumption, that "I am the body." In everyday life, it is expressed as "I am the body so and so who is or does such and such and owns this and that."

Somebody can say "I am Roger Bacon. I am a physical therapist. I own a house in Palm Springs, California." Okay, Roger is a physical therapist. Everybody gets that. Everybody is comfortable with that. But if we remove the hidden assumption that Roger is his body, if Roger lets go of his assumption that he is his body, if he stops identifying with the "I am the body" mastermind thought and its individual and global hypnosis, then the whole thing just falls down like a house of cards in a strong gust of wind. If there is no "Roger" body, then the rest is fiction. It is totally destroyed.

Another way to put it is the first question gets answered as "I am the I of the body" and the second question gets answered as "I am the I of the I" which is, of course, pure unbounded true "I."

At first, you will not notice that it is unbounded. When you get the second response, you focus on the pure feeling of first person "I-ness." This is the pure essence of your natural true Identity feeling. You will think it is a limited "I" but you will feel relief, a gap of silence.

At some point it becomes obvious to you that this pure essence I-feeling is free standing. It stands independent of and prior to the body. In this essence of pure Identity feeling, no limits are felt. No boundaries are felt. No restriction or contraction is felt. It is self-liberated and self-liberating. But this happens only when the Self itself rises up and conquers thought. After conquering many other thoughts, the Self finally captures the I-thought and destroys it.

In my sadhana, I had become aware that the I-thought was arising from the Heart on the right. So I was inquiring with the awareness that it was coming from there. So when I asked "Where are you coming from?" I already knew the answer. The bottom line is that what you really are is the pure feeling of limitless being. You are unbounded being without any limitations at all. This is an ever new joy because it is sourced from within itself. It is the natural freedom that we all intuitively sense is our birthright.

All of the worldly thoughts surround and protect this "I am the body" mastermind thought like a gang of cold-blooded criminals. They will defend their gang boss to the death. These thoughts are hard-hearted and they do not care about your happiness.

At the center, like a spider in a web, lurks the "I am the body" thought. It is dedicated to confining and limiting your ability to know, feel and enjoy your unlimited thought-free pristine nature.

It is like trying to make love wearing a suit of body armor like a medieval knight. No matter what you do or how you try, you will never get the natural real experience. The hard plate of thoughts hides our deep bliss. The Self is pure Identity feeling without any restriction or limitation whatsoever. The feeling that we human beings have of being me or I is based upon the Identity feeling of the Self, but it is mistakenly assigned, in powerful stealth hypnosis, to the body.

The body is believed to be the basis for our feeling of existing, of our continuous unbroken feeling of being me or I. But this is a terrible error and it has created this prison planet. Ultimately it is not dictators or some other mysterious force that confines and limits we the people and keeps us down. It is our ignorance, our thinking we are the physical body.

We were all born as royal kings or queens, as rulers, as masters of all that we survey. We throw that away and instead take on the dirty torn rags of the lowly downtrodden servant. Then we wander the world in search of a mysterious precious something that we know we should have. But we cannot quite put our finger on what that something is.

Well, that mysterious "something" that everybody is searching for is the Self, their true Self. The very nature, the essence of the Self is pure unalloyed happiness, peace, love and well-being. It is the experience of unadulterated pure good feeling. This is the happy essence feeling we were much closer to as a child. The Self is regal and royal. It is the true ruler, the King or Queen of the world. Until you regain that feeling and receive your royal inheritance, you will never be completely happy. Thought game after thought game may entertain you, but lasting happiness escapes you.

It is the experience of many, once they get on the path of meditation, that their best moments, their moments of greatest happiness or peace or joy or love, are not when they make a lot of money or acquire something. These best of the best moments occur exactly when the mind is the most quiet, when there is a deep silence of the mind, when the thoughts are quiescent. Then it is like something comes forward, something that was hidden, and this something is pure formless joy-happiness-peace. That something is the Self. It is the real Holy Grail. It is the supreme Prize. It is the pure Gold.

After this success with silencing the mind, some people get the idea to latch onto the silent mind. They work hard to keep a silent mind at all times. The mind will never be silent. The Self is already Silence.

So when you realize the Self, you live in this natural untouched Silence all the time. Thoughts come and go. They are of no consequence. So do not hold onto the top layer of superficial silence. Keep digging. Uncover the Silence of the Self hidden under the I-thought.

The world for most people is a thought prison with many hardened layers of thought confining them like multiple straight jackets. At the heart or core of this multi-layered confinement is the "I am the body" thought who brilliantly operates with many clever deceptions like a mastermind criminal mob boss. The so-called "world" that people see is a dark twisted version of what the world really is. The world is actually the Self, it is actually pure Light and Love and Peace. It is Eden or Heaven. We have heard of Eden and Heaven. They are here but the I-thought covers them up.

Seen through the cold indifferent pitch black madness of constant thought confinement and bombardment, the world is a difficult even horrible place. It is a war zone fought with thought bullets and thought bombs. We have been blessed with a creative imagination, yet it gets twisted into books and movies that celebrate sadistic abuse, torture and killing.

Nobody is immune to death. Kings die. Billionaires die. Nobody gets out of here with what they acquired at the bodily level.

Everybody must give it up and let it go. We let go of our physical body and what goes on can be called "the soul." If you take the investigation all the way, this essence of this soul is found out to be the boundless unlimited joyful true Self. This perfect no-thought Self is who and what we really are. But that which hops from body to body and life to life is the I-thought.

That sounds like non-dualistic thriller fiction. It has a conspiracy theory flavor. I've always wondered why the world is the way it is. I've noticed that the more I think about the world and its problems, about my problems, the heavier and more difficult it all becomes. I know that I have the power to think myself into a depression state!

Those are good observations. That is how everything is worked out. Whatever I say needs to be investigated so that you can see it for yourself, test it and make it your own. There is nothing to believe. You are not being asked to have faith. You must resonate with it. Do your own observation. Conduct your own investigation. Keep a journal of your insights and experiences. Write down the date so that you can review your journey and see your progress.

At the foundation of doing this is your desire to be totally free and happy. If you keep drilling deeper and deeper, you will eventually get to the place where it all opens up. You will finally "strike oil" and you will be "rich." Then you will see what it is like to live without thought, to live as a human being and be free. Until you see that, thought is your king, your ruler and your slave master. Thought runs your life. Thought is your cruel hard-hearted boss.

But as I was saying, this is not a vague situation. It is not a mystery. I have spelled out the formula like a treasure map. It's not just my opinion. All of my main points are backed up by Ramana Maharshi, especially as amplified by a lesser known realized sage who was a beloved devotee of Ramana. This other man was Sri Sadhu Om. He is the author of *The Path of Sri Ramana: Part One* which explains Self-inquiry in very practical and specific steps.

If the battle with the mind meant that we would be constantly fighting thousands of thoughts every day, the war would be lost. But this onslaught of thoughts is a deception. Behind the confusing mental barrage there is but one thought, the dictator thought, the mastermind thought, the crime boss thought, the expert criminal thought. He has many gangs and he sends them out to harass you, beat you up and scare you. Human crime bosses and the I-thought have much in common!

There is a single thought to which the dark power of the false cruel kingdom of thought can be traced. This "evil" king of thought is the "I am the body" idea aka the "I-thought." The mind works very hard to disguise the fact that behind the seemingly endless onslaught of limiting thoughts there is but one central "boss" thought. If you investigate it directly and don't give up, you will see this truth for yourself. As long as you think you are the body, you will suffer.

If you can soften or let go of that idea for even a short time, you will see for yourself that the mind is just a bundle of thoughts. Like a bundle of sticks, the sticks can be burned in a fire one stick at a time. When the sticks are burned up, the bundle is gone. But until you identify and capture the clever mastermind deceiver thought behind all of the other thoughts, especially the second and third person thoughts, these thoughts multiply and seem to go on forever.

If you are going to win a war against a difficult enemy, you must cut his lines of supply. If you allow him to keep getting new supplies and keep building new weapons of destruction, you will never defeat him. You must find his weakness and cut off his life support. You must cut through his lines of supply. Or you can think in terms of a big-time criminal who has finally been cornered in his secret hideaway. You must smoke him out, get him to expose himself.

As long as you think "I am so and so who does such and such for a living in this external physical world" then you will be searching for happiness and never find it. You must come to understand that the "I am so and so" that starts out your false identity statement is an assertion of the false claim that "I am the physical body which has been named so and so."

It always comes down to this: "I am the body." Who cares what you call it? Entertainers change their name, change the name of the body, and nobody cares. It enhances their career. So what is the continuous key? It is claiming that "I am the body."

But the basis for the feeling of continuous identity is not the body. The body is fragile and temporary. It is an always changing machine. How could it be the source of identity?

Science has studied the body through and through. It has not found a self in it. The special feeling of existing, of being, of having a precious unique original identity, is based on the Self. It is not based on the body. This is what you must see for yourself.

Once you see it clearly, then you can stabilize in it. After you are stabilized in it, you will be happy and free. You will have the peace that surpasses understanding. This is the highest good.

Thoughts will come and go, but they will be like tiny musical birds or gentle wispy clouds in a vast beautiful wide open sky. Although thoughts are required for human functioning, these thoughts are not yours. These thoughts are operated by the Cosmic Central Computer, meaning that they are from the Self. Live in a state of not-knowing like a child. A thought comes. A thought goes. Who cares?

Thoughts can be good servants but they are terrible masters. You, the aware pure Self, must take the place of the body-based I-thought as the true Master. You must be the master of all of your thoughts and to do that, you must be that which is totally beyond and superior to thoughts. That which is beyond all thoughts has a name. It is the Self.

Amrita Nadi and the Heart on the Right

Ramana talked about the sacred spiritual Heart on the right. It remains poorly understood. Some people experience it. Other people don't. It is a spiritual reality. More and more people are having the experience of the Heart on the right. When they do, it is a deep inspiration. It is a very positive experience.

Ramana never told people to concentrate on a point of the physical body in order to arouse a feeling of the Heart on the right. Even so, such a feeling or a vision may arise there in the course of Self-inquiry meditation. If it does, it is a good sign. It should not be dismissed or ignored.

If you are experiencing the Heart in the right in some way, it is a good idea to see a teacher who knows about it and has experienced it. Sometimes the experience of the Heart on the right is uncomfortable. The I-thought is fighting and trying to discourage you by giving you painful sensations. If this is happening. definitely find a good teacher. The fact that the I-thought is fighting you so fiercely means you are close to success.

What was Ramana Maharshi talking about when he referred to the Heart on the right? Other people haven't seen that. Nisargadatta Maharaj said he greatly respected Maharshi's realization but that he had not had any experience of this Heart on the right.

It is perhaps a subject of controversy that Sri Ramana Maharshi talked about the Heart on the right. But he is not the only one who has experienced it. Many of his disciples have. I have experienced it many times. I know from my own experience that it is the local reference point in the physical body of the Self.

If I look right now I can see the Heart on the right. It glows like a beautiful happy golden sun. It is right there and easy to see. Not only that, its radiance is the Source of the physical world. When I look at the world I see the world, but I also see the Heart, the Self.

You can see it right now? How do you know it is not just your imagination?

The whole world and everything in it is "just your imagination." What I am talking about is a direct subjective experience of the Source that is related to the causal body. The physical heart on the left chest is related to the physical body. The subtle heart in the center of the chest is related to the subtle or astral body. The causal Heart on the right of the chest, a few finger widths from the center of the chest, is related to the causal body. It is the domain of silent seamless bliss and deep regenerating sleep.

All of these apparent levels are co-existing and simultaneous. We are talking as physical bodies right now, but at this very same time our dream level of being is active and involved. Our causal level of being is active and involved. That ultimate level of being which is called the Self is fully present, fully participating. All the levels of existence are here right now in this conversation. For each of these levels, the physical, the astral and the causal, there is a heart. For each of these levels, there is a body. There is a physical body, an astral body and a causal body.

In terms of a physical marker or noticing that can be felt as a sensation, the place at the nipple level just to the left of the right nipple on the chest is the location for sensing the causal body. It is the spot where perception of the natural Radiance of the Self may take place for those who are aware of the Self in the waking state. It is not a requirement, but it may happen. It did to me. But the Heart or Self is not limited to or stuck in the body. It is All and Everything.

That is something else that is controversial. The idea that the Self can be represented by the physical body somehow. This marker that you are talking about. Some would say it is a distraction, maybe even a false teaching.

It can be a distraction if you make it an object of seeking. But if it arises as a natural outcome of your process, of working to reach the roots of the mind and arrive at the Self upon the destruction of the "I am the body" thought, then I would say it is okay. In fact, it is a wonderful fulfillment, a thrilling and beautiful confirmation of your spiritual success.

After all, what you experience is what you experience. It is what I experienced and there was no effort on my part for that to be so. I am not saying concentrate on the Heart on the right like a chakra center. I am saying do Self-inquiry meditation and it may arise spontaneously for you. Or it may not. Either way, it is what is right for you.

There was a wonderful Self-realized teacher called A. Ramana, an American, who passed away recently. He experienced the Heart in the same way as I do. He described the same thing in almost the same words. You can feel the pure joy and the love that is there, that radiates from there. It is the Source of Radiance. There is a little-known yoga that can arise. It is the yoga of the Heart and of the Amrita Nadi that goes down from the Crown and arrives in the Heart on the right.

Apparently, the experience is not that common. But I experienced it and my experiences, which came on their own, match that which is described by Sri Ramana Maharshi, A. Ramana and other Self-realized persons. So I feel pretty secure in its validity.

In this enlightenment, the Amrita Nadi, the "River of Immortality," blazes and the Light of the Self expands to include everything. Then everything disappears as an object and becomes translucent due to the Light of the Self. This is also known as "the light of a thousand suns." So en-light-enment is an accurate description. You can still experience the world, but it is known to be Light.

You say that you have experienced the Amrita Nadi talked about by Ramana Maharshi?

Not only have experienced it but I am experiencing it. It is right here right now. It is forgotten in terms of an exclusive passageway, but the transformation into transcendental luminosity still applies. You could say that the flowering of Amrita Nadi is being experienced. It is true for everybody, but not everybody is consciously experiencing it.

The Crown chakra at the top of the head is the destination of Kundalini yoga. Some people go to above the head, to very subtle chakras up there. But it all boils down to the same thing, that the Crown is thought of as the goal.

For some this works fine. I think the Heart on the right — we shall just call it the Heart, since the physical attribution is not needed — the Heart works as a silent partner. It does not crave the recognition. It is fine with being totally silent and invisible. So the authentic realization takes place but the Heart as such is never noticed. However, some other realizers, and this is true in traditions around the world, do notice that there is a causal Heart and they experience it in some form.

What I found is that the Crown is the natural highest point, it is the Mount Kailash which is associated with Lord Shiva. I had a major Kundalini awakening at the age of 16 and Kundalini has been a big factor in my life, but on and off.

Finally, Mother Kundalini did take me up to the Crown, to the peak of manifestation there. I went through a progressive process that I was able to read about and identify as a traditional Kundalini path.

Towards the end of this Kundalini journey up to Mount Kailash, I actually found a book that described everything I had experienced. In this Kundalini tradition, it said you stopped at the Crown chakra. It also said you could get stuck on your way up in Ajna, the third eye chakra, because there was a major block there. (4)

But after I got to the Crown and stabilized there, I discovered that this highest point in the Crown has a secret passageway down to the deepest hidden source, the Cave of the Heart. So when I investigated the source of the true Silence at the Crown, I found that there is a route that descends to the Heart.

What I mean is that I did not first go looking for the Heart. Doing a spontaneous Kundalini yoga combined with Self-inquiry, I worked my way up to the Crown. But then once I was established there, I had the intuition of the Heart. I saw the Amrita Nadi.

To be exact, I saw it rise up from the Heart on the right. It was not like I was at the top of the head and found some fixed inner road. It rose up like a living silent joyful Song of Light. When I think of how it rises up, I am reminded of the mythical Fountain of Youth.

It looks like a bright glowing ribbon or living river of bright white light that is a half-spiral from the top of the head. From the Crown, It passes down behind the head and then to the front of the body. Or you can think of it as going up from the Heart on the right, from the causal center, up to the head.

This is the path of the I-thought to the head. It goes across the chest to include all three hearts — the physical, the astral and the causal. It has been observed by many others. I discovered it for myself but it is not my discovery.

Let's say I accept that you see these things which are, as you say, validated by Ramana. What is their meaning? Why does it matter? Isn't the Self formless and universal?

If you are not experiencing it, and from your questions it sounds like you are not, then you may think it is some arbitrary thing, something that got added on to gussy it all up. It may seem that way, but it is not like that at all. The experience of the World as the Self is a glorious experience. Everything is the Heart and everything is Light. The Heart is central to all of this. So any experience of the Heart or Amrita Nadi is welcome.

It is not some kind of attachment. It is a celebration, a dancing of the joy of Being. I believe it was Sri Ramana Maharshi who compared the Crown to the moon and the Heart to the sun. I would say that matches my experience. There is a relationship between them.

I would say that the Crown reflects the Heart. The spiritually realized Crown chakra is basically the fully functional but purified mind that is free of the "I am the body" idea. So whether you realized via Self-inquiry or Kundalini yoga or devotional bhakti yogi or some other path, the destruction of the "I am the body" thought has to take place for you to truly realize the Crown.

So the Crown is the functioning yet silent mind that is a no-mind. The Heart is the center of Being itself, the eternal Support, the empty Center of the Wheel around which everything spins. It is the utterly silent home where there is no mind at all and never has been a mind. Ramana referred to the moon that can be seen during the daytime. This is the Crown when it is functioning as the silent mind. The Crown is like a supercomputer and the Heart is like the hidden ultimate power source that powers this supercomputer.

When we are using a computer, we are not thinking about the power unless there is a problem. Likewise, when the pure silent mind at the Crown is functioning there does not have to be a remembering of the Heart which is its power source. Remember, too, that the Crown is something that is known. So everybody who studies Kundalini or yoga learns about the Crown and knows where it is. Can the ultimate truth be something that everybody knows so easily?

I don't think so. I think the ultimate truth will remain hidden. Any fool can put his attention at the top of his head and think he has realized something great. The Heart is subtler than subtle. The Heart is the root. The Crown is the Flower with a thousand petals.

The Heart is the Light of a thousand suns. Amrita Nadi is the stem that connects the Heart Root and the Crown Flower. This is the secret pathway of immortality. Sri Ramana Maharshi says so. I also say this based on my own experience. There is nothing beyond it.

You Cannot Get Enlightened (Because You Already Are)

Identification with the mind leads to a wild goose chase that will never end. The more you pursue the chimeras of the mind, the more you find there is to pursue. The only answer is to STOP!

When you stop, you find that the mind is not what you thought it was. It is like being addicted to a toxic substance. You think you can't live without it. You think this is the only way to live. Yet if you are lucky enough to break free of it, when the sun rises in the morning and clarity dawns, you see it all with fresh eyes. You realize you were living in a state of addiction, a state that was not healthy. You were out of balance, crazy even.

The word "healthy" is closed related to the word "wholeness." It is common for people to talk about this part of themselves and that part of themselves, but what is that? All of that is just thoughts. There are no parts. There is only YOU... and you are the seamless whole. In this wholeness that you are lives forever the peace, love and happiness that you desire.

It's a popular notion in the Advaita community that you cannot get enlightened. You can prepare for it but you cannot make it happen. The ego cannot get rid of itself. So just let go. Relax into awareness. Give up your struggle.

That's true, but my reasons for agreeing may be different than the usual ones. I have a different model based on my own experience which is that the Self, the Heart, is calling you to be your True Self.

This feeling of pure Being that is your True Self is apparently limited by the ego notion which in turn depends completely on the "I am the body" idea. This body-identification idea is false. It can never be real.

Your chances of realizing all of this and arriving at the pure unbounded existence feeling of the Self are slim if you don't do any practice. When you do Self-inquiry, although in the beginning and perhaps for a long time it feels like "you" are the one "doing" it, in fact it is the supreme Self that is doing it. The Self is meditating you, the one who thinks they are the body. The Self is dissolving that you into nothingness, but this nothingness turns out to be the fullness of the Self. You will die as the body-based small self, but you will be reborn as the universal "big I" true Self.

So you are saying to people that they should meditate, that the sustained effort at doing meditation over time is in fact the avenue through which the Self will work on their ignorance and liberate them in their life?

Yes, that is well said. If you don't do any meditating, if you don't do any Self-inquiry, if you don't make the effort, then you will not build the bridge that is needed for the Self to cross into your waking state and brighten your daily life awareness. The Self ever is, but the experience of the Self depends upon the purity of the mind.

Ultimately, the mind is eliminated completely, either in terms of it being an obstacle or in the sense of it actually being destroyed. The mind is a fabulous time and space machine, but the Self is beyond time and space.

As impressive as the mind is, it is dualistic. We see this with technology. These new inventions from the mind create as they destroy and destroy as they create. They are always a mixed blessing. They keep changing and changing.

It turns out there is no stability in the mind. This is what you see. The inventors of the machine gun thought their new and terrible weapon would usher in world peace. How wrong they were. That is the trickery of the mind.

Either way, whether it is dead or just permanently disabled, the mind is no longer causing any interference with the seeing, feeling, hearing, sensing, intuiting and knowing of the Self.

The experience of the Self is direct, unbroken and undeniable. So the statement that "You cannot get enlightened" is true in a couple of ways.

But how I mean it is still not going to be the way a lot of other people mean it. The Self is already enlightened. The one who is the body is not enlightened, but that is the one who must disappear if the Self is going to appear. That is why we challenge the I-thought in meditation. We do not just passively watch thought. We are the Self asserting itself.

It is true in the sense that the you that you think you are as the experience "I am the body" cannot get enlightened because it is what is going to die. So in order for the real You to step forward, the sneaky, deceptive body-obsessed I-thought must get flushed down the toilet! The Self becomes supremely aggressive finally and actually destroys the I-thought.

There are no two ways about this. The "I am the body" thought must die. It must go and be gone forever. Only then the Sun of the Self rises to Illuminate everything and put an end to the false darkness. The "I am the body" thought is an eclipse of the spiritual sun.

The other way in which I feel that statement is true is that in the process, the apparent journey, to Self-realization, whether it is through Self-inquiry meditation or some other means, "you" are not the one doing the sadhana. The Self is doing it. The Self is pulling you into the Self from the inside and pushing you towards the Self on the outside.

When it happens, it was never the mundane body-based "you" that did it. It may seem that way, but it is not that way. You as the Self did it. You as the Self, as your real You, will be the one who kills the false "you," the body thief.

So you would agree that I cannot get enlightened if the I that I am referring to is the body-based small self. And you would agree on the basis that the enlightenment process is the work of the Self, not the body-based I. Is that correct?

Yes, that's correct. The body-based "I" is just a fiction. It is literally like the character in a novel or movie. It has no real existence apart from the attention that is given to it. You see that in the media. A character, such as vampires, gets attention in the movies. Vampires are very big in our media and culture right now.

But if everybody stops thinking about vampires, then they will just go away. It will be like they never existed. They never did truly exist except in the minds of those who gave to that idea the valuable nutrition of their attention.

The body-based "I" is not the doer. It was never the doer. The only one who can do the spiritual work is the Self. It is a paradox but the Self is the real doer. Even though it is said that the Self does nothing, the Self does the sadhana.

One way to resolve this paradox is to think of the doing that you do in a dream. In a dream you perform various actions and have experiences. Where does it all go when you wake up? These things seemed very real at the time, at the level of the dream. But now that you have awakened, now you know it was just a dream. So you might say "Now I know it was not real. I experienced it but it was only a dream."

Not only that, it was all cooked up in your brain. Your body never went anywhere. So it was a fantasy, but very real to you on a subjective level. There was even a feeling of it being physical to the touch and three-dimensional in the dream state.

You can argue that in dreams some people astral travel and so on, but that is not relevant here. Our so-called physical reality is a similar dream state only at a heavier density. This is why some Self-realized persons can do miracles that transcend three-dimensional time and space. What you can do in your dreams they can do in this world.

Jesus is famous for manifesting the wine, loaves and fishes out of nothing. We do this in a dream without effort and without giving it any thought. We just think of something in the dream and there it is.

It seems normal. For a Master like Jesus, this world is just a dream. Instant manifestation in the world dream is just as easy and effortless. Others get fascinated by manifestation but it is better to realize the Self. Forget about secret powers.

There is a paradox here. You might think "Why doesn't somebody like Jesus become a billionaire?" The paradox is resolved because when you know it's all a dream, you don't care about it. Even the money is just a dream! It is not really real.

Also, if manifestation is so easy, then you can just manifest what you need when you need it. Why get weighed down by bank accounts, corporations and taxes if you don't need to? Just go straight to producing the desired result when the demand arises.

So there are benefits, so to speak, to realizing the Self. But the Self is already realized. The lamp is already turned on. The Light is already shining. We just have to remove the false covering over it and there it is. It is our beloved birthright.

This false covering over the Light of the Self is the "I am the body" idea, the I-thought. This idea is what must die or be completely removed and discarded in order for the real You to be born, to arise in all its glory. Jesus said "Don't hide your light under a bushel." This is what he meant. The bushel or bucket, the covering, is the I-thought.

Until awakening happens, it may be very difficult to understand. Just ask yourself "Am I experiencing the highest most stable peace and happiness I am capable of?" By that, I really do mean the very highest fulfillment that you can conceive of.

If you are not, then you need to dig deeper. Keep digging and eventually you will find the Self. You will uncover the Truth by removing all of the false coverings that were hiding it. We all want to be happy. The Self IS happiness! The Heart is the quintessence of happiness!

Because we yearn from the Heart, we are not satisfied with this global junkyard. The Heart is the only pure gold. The rest is fool's gold. It is garbage wrapped up like a valuable present. Without peace and love, what is there? Peace and love are the Heart.

You the seeker must die in this process, but like the classic story of the caterpillar becoming the butterfly, the pure essence of "I-ness" that informed your body-based sense of existence will show itself to be an unbroken continuity at the realization of the unbounded Self. That same feeling of being the first person "I" is there, only now it is not limited in any way. You know it is you, the real you, and you know that you were this true you all along.

There is not the old me and now suddenly this new grand me that has no connection to the old you. No, the connection is obvious. This is you, the King unbound, the King without demeaning binding chains. No more is there me and you. There is no "other" at all. You are now the supreme First Person "I" that you always were but somehow had forgotten. There is only the one "I" or "I-I." This universal "I" is experienced everywhere as everything. When you think "I" or feel "I" you know that it refers to everything. You know that you as "I" are everything. You are all. Words are not adequate for this.

Just to be perfectly clear, when I say there is only this "I" that is exactly what I mean. Although you can still function in the world and interact with it, there is in fact no world. There is only the Self. You experience what people are calling the "world" but to you it is just the Self. You know the world dream is only a dream while you are still in it. But even calling it a dream is misleading. It is a paradox. Even though you can live and work in the world, it is not really there for you. People study and explore dreams. There is NO world to study and explore. There is ONLY the Self.

The Self is the supreme source of joy. You can be just sitting on a park bench and that is the ultimate. You are already everything. How are you going to add to that? The answer is that there is nothing to add to that. It is full and complete.

In fact, it is more than full or complete. In the sacred texts, it is described as ever-full and overflowing, so even if there is an expenditure, a giving out, from the Self, the Self is still just as whole and complete and full as it ever was. This is why the search finally comes to an end. What is there to search for? You are totally full. You are everything there is.

The butterfly that arose from the caterpillar of seeking is set free to be without limits, without fear. You are Love and everything is Love and You know it. You are Love incarnate. You are Love dancing the joy of pure Being. You are LOVE dancing with everyone and everything and, at the same time, you ARE everything and everyone.

People hear this and think "Oh, then you radiate incredible love all of the time." I can only speak for myself. I do not radiate incredible love. Radiate love to whom? I am already That. Not just me, you and everybody are already That.

People hear this and they think "Oh, you must be in a state of ecstasy." No, it may sound paradoxical but ecstasy is less. This peace is supreme. This peace is paramount.

Ramana talks about deep bliss as total absorption takes place. Normal duties are no longer attended to. The person is absorbed in the Radiance of the Self. However, as he pointed out, these are levels of bliss due to purification of residual mind continua. Self-realization is not based on bliss. It is based on dropping body-identification.

Do You Sincerely Want To Be Free?

The great modern sage Sri Nisargadatta Maharaj is well-known for saying that being earnest is an important factor in realizing Truth. The reason is that what you will attain in this life will be based on what you care the most about.

Jesus said "Where your heart is, there will be your treasure also." Nisargadatta is saying the same thing. If in your heart you are fully committed to realizing your True Self, if it is honestly more important to you than anything else, then you have a very good shot at attaining it in this lifetime.

It is not possible to achieve this without Grace, but Grace is always given to one who makes the sincere sustained effort. The paradox is that it will not happen without effort, but your effort does not cause it. Your effort "qualifies" you for the liberating Grace.

You may fool yourself and fool others, but you will not fool God. God knows what it is in your heart. Actually, God is in your Heart. That is the journey — from the troubled and yearning yet earnest human heart to the boundless thought-free pure spiritual Heart.

I want to be free. What do I need to do?

There is no set path, but the ingredient that seems to be common to all Self-realizers is that they are very sincere, very earnest and very honest, especially with themselves. It isn't just hard work or effort or the number of hours spent on the meditation cushion. There needs to be a core quality, a heart quality, of deep genuine earnestness.

Are you talking about how people think that just doing a technique over and over will do it? All I have to do is find the right secret technique, the special glittering magic method.

Yes, that's implicit in what I am saying. My point is that you cannot fake it to make it. You cannot fool the Self. In modern psychological terms, you are becoming more authentic.

Obviously, you cannot become more authentic by lying to yourself. Even if nobody else knows that you are lying, you still know that you are lying. Your heart knows that you are lying. Living a life of lies will keep you away from the Self, for the Self is the Heart and it knows.

Even if everybody else thinks you are the real deal, if deep inside you know you are phony, you can be sure the Self knows it, too. It knows it and it will discount your efforts to realize it. The Self cannot be deceived. So the earnestness is in terms of being willing to tell the truth, to be totally even brutally honest with yourself. You will leave no stone unturned in your investigation of the Truth. You will investigate and inquire and study and dig until you get to the very bottom of it all. You will never ever give up. It is the greatest and finest commitment a human being can make.

Realizing the Self sounds like the ultimate treasure hunt — fun, exciting, demanding, difficult — a search for buried treasure!

Yes! It is the biggest and best treasure hunt possible for us human beings. It is also the least known and the best hidden. There is no greater treasure, no hunt that is more difficult. A Hindu myth says the gods and goddesses didn't want people to quickly and easily find the Self because if they did, they would become even greater than the deities. The gods and goddesses would instantly lose their status and they didn't want that.

So they figured out that the best place to hide this precious jewel of truth was in the heart. They knew that people would go looking all over the world and in their relationships and follow the success experts with their books and seminars and forget to look into their own hearts. So the Self is hidden in the Heart. It can be felt in the psychic heart chakra that is in the center of the chest and connected to the spine, but this subtle center is but an echo of the Heart on the right. The true Self can be said, in terms of the physical body, to live in the causal Heart on the right. This is its signature or felt sign in terms of the body.

Do you recommend meditating there, focusing the mind on the physical location of the Heart of the right?

The scholars and traditionalists in the Ramana Maharshi camp frown upon it. They say that it reinforces body identification. My experience with it is sort of in-between. As I did my Self-inquiry practice, which in my case was coordinated with being taken by the Kundalini to the Crown chakra, I became aware that there was an exchange going on between the Crown and the Heart on the right. So the Heart had called me to pay attention to it, and to do so at that location just to the right of the center line exactly where Ramana said it would be. The obvious right thing to do at the time was to pay attention there and abide there and fully BE there.

I have meditated on chakras like the Third Eye. Could you meditate on the Heart on the right in the same way?

To just do it out of the box with no previous experience with Self-inquiry, I would say there is no great harm in it, but I would not expect anything special to happen. Some people get results by concentrating on body locations with Kundalini and the chakras in the front. The causal Heart center is more subtle. The causal is related to the deep sleep state. The front chakras are related to the dream state which is more familiar and easier to contact.

So if it emerges in your experience, I would work with it. Feel free to experiment with it if you like. After all, it could be the Self that is calling you to do that. Ultimately, you are the Self, so you should listen to yourself and follow your own intuition. I would not avoid it just because of what was said in a book. But also I would not cook it up into some big special practice. It is an aspect of the Heart sadhana. The Heart is our intuition. This process is very intuitive.

I have seen it in students, the Heart and Amrita Nadi. I can tell when they have been activated, when they are "live." Then I know this person is a good candidate to achieve Self-realization. The ultimate outcome, though, is still in the hands of the Lord. In most cases, realization requires Grace. As the saying goes, God helps those who help themselves.

The Heart and the Amrita Nadi showed up for me. That much I know, which validates it for me.

But the common ingredient for all is to get back to the heart-felt earnestness and sustain that sincerity. That is the key. If you are meant to experience the Heart on the right, to see and feel its luminosity and its joy as an experience of spiritual yoga, then you will. It will add to your life and to your sadhana. It will be a valuable step and inspiration on the way.

Whatever is meant for you is bound to happen. Bringing your whole heart into your life, living with sincerity, gratitude and earnestness, that is what will open up new frequencies of possibility. Though we have a destiny, we have a choice as to what level we will live that destiny. When we live it at a higher level, then it is changed. Karmas get mitigated. Grace gets activated. The hidden spiritual opportunity that is hiding at each twist and turn of life is made available.

When we live our destiny from the highest level, which is the graceful spontaneity of the Self, then we release all the good to be with us now. We set free the total healing, the complete cleansing. The karmas unwind and get eliminated. Then the bliss and the radiant sense of fulfillment, peace and ease grows and grows.

Whatever we may believe, even if we are atheists, we only have one option which is to be our self. The atheist can realize just like anybody else. The atheist is the Heart right now, as are we all. There are no limits to the Heart.

According to the way of Ramana, that option is best fulfilled by realizing the Self, the Heart. The answer to "Who am I?" is "I am the Heart." There is no thought, no thinking of any kind, in the Heart. It is free of all limitation of any kind. It is Freedom itself. To be the Heart is to be fully free and completely happy. From deep within, we all yearn for this.

Enlightenment Is Simple (But That Doesn't Mean It's Easy)

Many approach Self-inquiry meditation as a mental technique. It is not mental at all. The identity that you have right now is real to you because you can feel it. If your sense of identity, of existing, of being you, was just like another passing thought, it could not possibly have the significance that it does to you. It could not function as the foundation of your life. Even though this is a strong clue, it is rare to understand this.

The light within this feeling of existing as "me," this feeling of being, quite literally is the Self. However, it has been put in prison. It is in jail. The jail cell is this physical body. But the body is not the problem. The mind's identification with the body is the error. The body is just the willing victim. It has no choice in the matter.

Enlightenment is realizing the true nature of this feeling of being, of this "I." The paradox is that you live in and as the truth but you think you don't have it. It is like living as a street person with amnesia when you're the son or daughter of the President. The moment you know the truth about your identity, about your real "I," everything instantly changes.

What is the single most essential point that gets missed?

That this experience of "I" that you are already having right now is IT! This "I" that you feel yourself to be right now is your real "I", only it has been confined and limited by thought.

This is not ultimately true, you are ever free and unbounded, but through the illusion of thought, that is the apparent experience — one of confinement, limitation, restriction, one of no love, no joy, no freedom, no light.

In short, due to the aggressive imposition of thought from an early age via global cultural conditioning, we are deeply unhappy. We are no longer in touch with who and what we are.

The journey back home can be thought of as having four stages: Recognizing, Remembering, Resting, Realizing. First you must recognize that the Self exists. Then you make the effort to remember the Self. Once remembering becomes natural for you, you can rest in the Self.

As resting in the Self becomes natural for you, sooner or later one or more breakthroughs occur and you find that you have realized the Self. You know "I Am That." You may oscillate between resting and realizing, but the realization becomes stable and then all of this becomes the mere memory of a misleading dream that never really existed. It becomes true for you that there is only the Self.

The experience of the Self that you recognize, remember, rest in and realize is the pure living feeling of unfettered Silence. This is your true identity free of thought. Unbounded pure feeling or being without any imposition by thought whatsoever is what you are. You are utterly prior to thought.

Once pure identity feeling is concentrated in itself without the imposition of thought, it discovers an ever new joy that is its very nature. Even though people typically pursue goals like money and possessions, happiness always turns out to be about having a good feeling, not collecting objects.

I feel that my sense of "I" is confined and limited. It is constricting and claustrophobic. I just want to get out of it and escape from it.

You describe the situation accurately as far as it goes, but you're also missing the real point. You describe the situation as it is conventionally experienced. I have a limited feeling or limited experience of my "I" so I want to get out of this "I" and into another "I". Or I want to change my "I" and upgrade it from an unhappy "I" to a happy "I".

What is being missed is that this "I" right now, your true "I", the "I" that you really are, is what you are right now. The thing to get rid of is not your "I", it's your deceptive lying thoughts. The sense of confinement and limitation is due to thoughts, no the "I" itself.

If you say so, but it is not my experience. I guess that is why I want to be different.

The tendency of the ego is to always go out, go somewhere else. The grass is always greener somewhere else. But it is not. The grass is greenest right here, in the unbounded "I". There is nowhere to go but here. Wherever you go, once you get there, it is here.

I'm not in a state of misery, but I know that a big piece of reality is missing for me. I guess you could say I am in the pursuit of happiness. I tried everything I knew about. I lived the fast lifestyle. I drank from the big cup, drained it dry and came up empty. I guess I'm asking you "What is the secret to happiness?" If you know, then please tell me.

The secret to happiness is that you are already happy! Happiness that is the result of changed circumstances or conditioned thoughts is not the real happiness. The real happiness has to be already within, already whole and complete, already fresh and new. It is like a spring in the ground. Mysterious and wonderful, the fresh water pours from it. Thoughts do not create it. They cover it.

Thanks, it's been great, I'll go now... I get that conceptually, but the experience is missing. I just don't feel it. I understand it mentally, but how do I go from unhappy to happy? I do see now that what I'm talking about and wanting is a feeling, not a concept or idea.

Yes, feeling, not emotion. Emotion is produced by thought. Feeling arises from within, from deeper than thought. Feeling is a form of pure intuition. The word "emotion" consists of "e-" meaning "out" and the word "motion." Thought stimulates a reaction that moves out. That is the I-thought moving out. The Self, pure awareness, does not move.

My situation is worse. I am honestly quite depressed. So I guess I am just very unhappy, to say it plain and simple. It's like I don't want to be me anymore. I would love to be somebody else. I feel super-confined by this me that I am supposed to be. Telling me that somehow deep inside I'm all happy and free is not giving me a warm fuzzy feeling.

Thanks for your input. Here is the straight-up answer right here and now: your "I", this "I" that you have right now and feel yourself to be right now, is your real "I", your true "I", but it is being confined. It is chained and in prison.

From a spiritual point of view, it is good that you feel this way, that you feel depressed. The agenda of the I-thought, of the false identity, is failing. Cracks are starting to appear in its armor, in its control over you. The trance is beginning to break. The whole thing is beginning to lose its appeal to you. That is a good thing. That is what has to happen.

Could you explain this prisoner thing, please? It sounds like a book or movie plot.

Yes, that is right. It is like that. It is the story of the hero, the real story of the hero. The analogy I like to use is that you were born the son or daughter of a billionaire, but you were switched at birth to extremely poor parents. They had many problems. The father was an alcoholic and beat his wife and so on. This is all on top of being broke. So you develop your own addictions and end up homeless and living on the street.

Sounds terrible. I guess my life could be worse.

There you are homeless, a street person. Your clothes are ragged, you haven't had a shower in weeks. Your hair is all matted. You are dirty and filthy. Your main goal in life is to get your drugs or your booze.

Then up walks a rich looking guy in a fancy suit. He speaks to you, saying your name. In your painful haze of toxic confusion, you shout at him and tell him to go away. But he persists.

He says your name again and announces "You probably won't believe me, but you are the son/daughter of a famous billionaire. You are his rightful heir. Now that you have reached the legal age, you can take your rightful place as his offspring and receive the vast wealth of your natural inheritance."

Here's the kicker. Because you were in reality born the son/daughter of this billionaire, all along this has been your true status. It is not something you could have invented or created for yourself. You had to be born into it. But because you really were born into it, the only thing you have to do, the only step you have to take, is to accept that this is your true identity.

Let go of the false idea that you are this limited street person. Embrace the unlimited feeling of being this super-wealthy person, a person who becomes wealthy by virtue of knowing their true identity in the Self.

Nothing else is required of you. Just accept who you are, be as you are, and you will have total freedom, happiness, love, joy and all of the rest. Being a billionaire is just a symbol for the Self that I am using because of the modern obsession with the monetization of everything.

So this is how the sage can say to you "I Am That" and it can be true of you right now. You are that. You were born that. This is the mystery of how you can say "I Am That" and still not be feeling it, not realizing it, not enjoying it. It is true but the realization of this truth is still waiting. The guru notifies you of your inheritance. But you must shake the cobwebs out of your brain and step forward to accept and embrace your real identity.

That's makes sense but your analogy breaks down because your homeless street person has somebody come to them and say "Just sign on the dotted line" and everything will be okay. I guess you are that person, or you could be that person for me, but I'm not seeing a paper with a dotted line. I am just seeing my homelessness and there is no way out of it.

Every analogy breaks down. Yes, I am the one who is reminding you that you are the heir of a spiritual billionaire. So what is the legal document which grants you access to your inheritance?

This step is a process, the process of reclaiming who you really are. You must drill down into the essential nature of this "I" that you are experiencing right now. Just as the acceptance of what this messenger is saying might be gradual for the street person, likewise is it likely to be gradual for you. At any rate, it does not usually happen the very first time you hear this idea. Signing on the dotted line is the sincerity, the earnestness.

So what is this process? How do I go from desperate and depressed homeless street person to happy spiritual billionaire person?

The short answer is that you do it through pure intuitive feeling. When I say you must drill down into your essential Self, I am talking about drilling down through layers of self-imposed thought. At the very bottom, at the root of all of these thought layers, is the "I am the body" thought or the "I-thought" for short. At the heart of this I-thought, giving it life, is pure I-feeling or "I Am" feeling.

The essential experience of your true "I" or real Self is one of being unlimited and unbounded. You do not feel any confinement whatsoever. You actually feel free. You feel that you are being yourself totally without any kind of restriction or limit or imposed notion or outer life obstacle.

The "I" feeling that you have now is the real "I" feeling, but its expansion as the totality of being has been stunted, conditioned and limited by thought, specifically by the "I am the body" thought. This belief that you are the physical body, drilled into you by society since you were very young, is the culprit.

It is always thought that imposes limitation. The positive thinkers and the Law of Attraction doers are on the right track, but they are trading iron chains of thought for golden chains of thought. Whether made of iron or gold, chains are still chains and the Self is not realized.

You are saying that if I get rid of the thought "I am the body," then I will instantly be the Self? I will automatically become enlightened?

Yes, that is true. But it's not like you can just throw it away. It is not usually quite that easy. It is more like this dense thought overlay, this thought density cover, gets dissolved over time. Insights gather and accumulate momentum as the innate Light of the Self brightens and brightens until finally the joyful supernal super-glow of the Self dissolves everything into itself.

When I think about this thought density imposition over the true unbounded pure "I" which each person really is, the image I consistently see is a big metallic mental cap. This cap is shaped like a bell or an upside-down bowl. In the unawakened person, it appears to be quite thick and made of dark hard metal. It sits on top of their head.

This bell-shaped cap is imposed upon the self-illuminated "I" at birth with the taking of the physical body. It covers the pure Light of the true "I." Coupled with the constant reinforcement from the culture, it goes unchallenged. "I am the body" is the constant hypnotic message of society.

The regular person has access only to the waking state and the dream state. The waking state imagination is roughly equivalent to the dream state, so the total conventional human experience is encapsulated in just the two states. We appear to move back and forth from them, from waking to dreaming, then dreaming to waking, in a constant flip-flop of different but similar states.

Our dreams and imagination are related to our waking life. Our waking life seems to be the source of our dreams. So the waking and dream states feed upon each other in a kind of false and deceptive cycle. It is false because it gives the illusion there is no exit.

But there is an exit, and that is via the deep sleep state. The deep sleep state is the state of perfect rest, but it contains the seeds of thought and embodiment. Ultimately, it is still a mixture. It is the transition state between the illuminated absolutely stable Self and the dream and waking states.

In the theater of the mind, it is the back door to the movie theater that has no lights on it. You don't see it unless you know to look for it. But when you go into this back door, there is only blackness, a featureless barren darkness. It is peaceful in a supremely silent way, almost like a graveyard — the silence of the unmoving dead.

It gives the appearance of being a blank and so appears to not be interesting. However, this is just another deception. This is the final layer of the covering. This blankness, inertness, dumbness or deadness is your ignorance.

When you penetrate that, you will get to the heart of the matter. You will arrive at the truth of your eternal identity. Though in darkness, you stand at the door of the Self which is the Supreme Spiritual Sun, the spiritual Holy Grail, the Light of Lights.

You may need to get comfortable with this darkness and learn how to live in that state of unknowing. Eventually this darkness melts away, perhaps very slowly, perhaps quickly.

As it does, the Light reveals itself more and more. At some point, you are amazed at the glory of this Light that you are and always were. You cannot believe you ever thought you were the body.

In fact, this ink black darkness is just a shroud, a covering. The Light of the Self is hidden behind the dark shroud. Behind it the Light of the Self blazes in all of its fullness, but you must go through the experience of blankness and of blackness, or at least I had to go through them. During this phase, I was told to forget everything, to drop all knowledge.

So people oscillate between waking and dreaming, but the real exit is in the dark and nobody is talking about it. Deep sleep seems to be blank and empty. In fact, there is an intelligence to this dense darkness. It is under cover of this darkness that the "I am the body" thought is hiding.

In the waking state, there is the feeling of being the body. In the dream state, if you pay close attention, there is the feeling of being the body. But that feeling is not found in the deep sleep state. You do not remember being the body there in any form. So the feeling of being the body must originate in and from the deep sleep state. This is what sages like Ramana Maharshi say.

The dark metallic bell that overlays the true "I", the cap that locks us into limitation via the "I am the body" thought, is that this causal pitch black darkness, too?

Yes, exactly. But it must be approached in the waking state by deep feeling. When you deeply investigate your "I" feeling, you find that the feeling in its pure state without thought interference is unbounded and unlimited. It tastes of freedom. It is your true "I".

This has been interesting. I have never heard this stuff before. But I am still confused as to what I should actually do. What should I do to realize this truth of myself?

Do not listen to your thoughts. They are from your "I am the body" thought confinement. Instead, enter into your "I" feeling in and of itself. Be your "I" feeling. Rest in your "I" feeling. Live from your "I" feeling. Inquire into the truth of your I-thought. Drop your thoughts. Forget thinking. Fly like a bird in a sky of no thought.

Turn away from secondary thoughts and return again and again to the primary thought. This is the I-thought. Isolate this I-thought and dwell in it. Its core, its heart, is this pure I-feeling. It is like a candle burning inside a locked room. Unlock the door. You find the candle already burning. As you study the I-thought day in and day out, you become a pure thoughtless witness to it. Your awareness grows until it is too big for the box. Then it explodes free.

When Ramana says "Be what you are... Be yourself and nothing more... to think is not your nature," he is saying "Be your pure 'I' feeling that is your birthright. Be it in its natural unconditioned state. Taste the unbounded freedom that is the feeling of I without thought." Let go of thought. Be beyond thought. Forget thought. Leave thought behind.

The mistake is in the thinking, and the first mistake in your thinking, which took place before you can remember, is the creation of the primary seed thought "I am the body." That evolves into "I am this body with this name with these parents living in this place doing these things" and so on. From this tiny seed grows the sweaty steaming jungle of the apparent dog eat dog world.

When you go beyond the waking and dreaming and face up to and work through the darkness of the causal body, then you find the Light of the Self. But you can do all of this from the waking state by dwelling in the purity of feeling. Thought is not your true nature. The ineffable Silence of pure unbounded feeling is your nature. When you dwell in this, everything is revealed.

Jesus said "Do not hide your light under a bushel." Well, a bushel is a basket and it looks a lot like the bell-shaped cap I see in my visionary way. I believe Jesus is saying that our Light is the Light of the Self, of our true nature. We should not cover it with the bell-shaped thought prison.

Do not hide this natural in-born Light that is our true inheritance under a basket, under the bell-shaped causal body imposition which at the root is the "I am the body" thought. In the waking and the dream states, being the body is taken as the given. So what is the source of this idea?

In the endarkened causal state, the "I am the body" thought lurks under cover of deep darkness like a master criminal. He must be exposed, meaning the causal body must be illuminated and dissolved into a transparency. Some even say it must be destroyed.

Then the Light of the Self shines forth. It was always there and always shining. This Light of the Self never went away. It is eternal. But it can and did get covered over by thought, or at least this is what seemed to happen. Ultimately, even that story is just more thoughts.

Be the Light of the Self by feeling your "I" feeling without the interference or imposition of any limiting, confining or defining thought. You are beyond definition. When you are defined, then you are made finite. You are not finite except in thought. In truth, in feeling, you are infinite.

You are unbounded freedom itself. Were it not for your thoughts, you would realize your Self right now. You Are That.... Here and Now.

Real lasting happiness is to be your true unlimited Self. It cannot be taken away from you. Life is one long identity crisis. Be what you really are. Claim your true identity.

You will have the answer to "Who am I?" when you die. Why not arrive at that answer now and be free of the whole thing?

If you did not get it before death, then death is a great opportunity. Any preparation made beforehand in meditation will be of great help when that time comes. Death will come to you. The body is given and then it is taken away. Be ready today. It could happen today.

Are You Sensitive Enough?

The sensitive person may see the world as brutal and indifferent. They may feel that the majority of people are insensitive blockheads who have tuned out the truth. Although this sensitivity seems to provide access to valuable insights, it comes at a price. The sensitive person is vulnerable and easily overwhelmed. They may be inclined to feel like a victim.

The answer to that dilemma is not to become less sensitive. The answer is to become more sensitive. What exactly are you being sensitive to? When this is investigated, it is found that a strong dualistic framework underlies the woes of the sensitive person.

Persistent and prolonged investigation of this conflicted dualistic scenario reveals that the pain and discomfort are not caused by external forces. They are not caused by the unfairness of life. Millions of people die at the hands of dictators, millions of children go without food, millions of good people struggle day in and day out just to survive.

Yet the sensitive person is not suffering from these harsh realities. They may think they are overwhelmed by the world, but the mechanism of suffering is within. It can be exposed in all its narcissistic glory only by becoming more sensitive, not less.

Become sensitive to every arising thought, every arising emotion, every arising sensation. Become sensitive to how this experience of separation, this existential agony of an isolated stranded separate self in a cold callous unfeeling world, got created in the first place. Become sensitive to what truly matters in a world where nobody survives, where everybody dies.

The world is overwhelming. It is so ugly, so brutal. I cannot deal with it.

Good.

Easy for you to say — good — you don't care. I am suffering every day. The world is so full of suffering. Don't you follow the news?

A little. Enough to know it is still there.

I think my problem is that I am too sensitive.

No, your problem is that you are not sensitive enough.

How can you say that? How can you know? You are not inside of my experience. You do not feel what I feel.

Sure, that's true. But I don't need to do that. Your sensitivity is still all about you. That is why it is still a problem for you. It is preserving your sense of self. That is its function.

Why would I torture myself like that?

Why would you torture yourself? The answer is in the question. You still get to be the focus. The ego still survives. It is still the center of attention. Your narcissism thrives.

If you were sensitive enough by my standards, then you would be sensitive enough to experience for yourself that the state of being separate, of having a separate existence, is incredibly profoundly painful. Instead, you are being self-indulgent, playing the victim.

But the world is ugly. Children are dying. The earth is getting polluted. Dictators kill millions of people. And it's getting worse.

Why this obsession with the world? The world does not care about you.

That's what I am saying. The world doesn't care. Nobody cares.

That's interesting. "Nobody" cares. I would say that is exactly right. It is "nobody" that cares. Those who think they are a "some body" of some kind, they are too preoccupied with being a body to truly care. They care about their body and that is all they care about.

That's not what I meant.

I know. But it is what I meant. Here's what I am trying to say. The world that you experience is just a reflection of you. When you realize that you are the source of the world, that you are the key to it all, then you will not be troubled by the world. It is your world. It is a play of light and shadow. Good and bad are two sides of the same mirror.

So it's all your fault!

Yes, I accept full blame for everything. I really screwed up!

But seriously, I don't see how you could create the world.

By create I mean I realize that I am the foundation for it. Without me, it does not exist. When you see the world for what it is, you no longer try to change it. It is a big machine and it runs by itself. It's got everything in it, all of the extremes, and it's function is to keep perpetuating itself. In its own way, it is absolutely perfect. Nothing is wrong with it.

Why would I want to interfere with a machine that is functioning perfectly when part of its perfection is that it is self-perpetuating and totally automatic?

Things are exactly the way they should be. There is no other way. How could there be? How can things be other than exactly the way they are?

But that takes me back to the suffering. All the innocent children who die of starvation, get abandoned by their parents, get kidnapped. It goes on and on. The world is a terrible place.

The world is a terrible place, it is a beautiful place, it is a neutral place. The world just is. It's not going anywhere. It's got it all. It is the ultimate buffet.

So you just don't care.

On the contrary, I care about what really matters. What really matters is to be sensitive to the very nature of the self that is reacting to all of this. If the world didn't suck so much, if it did not create this suffering for us, I wonder if any of us would wake up. The suffering is pointing to you, not to the world.

So you are saying I should be looking at me, not at the world?

Because you are sensitive enough to care about others and the world, you are suffering. Now you ask "Who is suffering?" That is the point.

I am suffering. I already know that.

Life itself is suffering until you examine the true nature of the separate self that is arising in you. To be separate in this way, to be a human being with a body who thinks that he or she is separate, this is the ultimate suffering. It is painful beyond comprehension. It makes being tortured in a Nazi prison camp a pleasant vacation by comparison.

That is why I say you are not sensitive enough. When you become sensitive enough in the way that I am speaking, then every moment of separate existence will feel like agony. It will be a loud horrible grating noise that you cannot ignore.

No matter what your pleasant experience — delicious food, a good sexual orgasm, a funny movie, a new drug — this agony of the separate self will be there. It will spoil everything. You will be forced to deal with it. That dealing with the pain of separation is called sadhana. That is the work, the right effort of seeking.

You will know you have a big problem. Wherever you go, there you are. Your life sucks. You are one big prickly painful bundle of pain, of sharp edges, of agony.

So you want to get rid of that self. But it is not that easy, as the self cannot get rid of the self. That is what dawns on you eventually. If you arrive at this point in an authentic way, then there is a chance that this search will become ripe enough that it can just fall away, like the ripe fruit from the tree. But if it is not ripe yet, then the seeking continues. It changes form and direction, but it is still seeking.

The genuine seeker has it right that he is the problem. He has gone beyond blaming the world. Self-inquiry, isolating the I-thought and knowing the truth of it, is the solution.

So I am letting the noise of the world overwhelm my ability to listen to myself, to the nature of what it is to be me moment to moment.

That's pretty good. I like that.

So what do I do?

When I studied with Ramesh Balsekar, he was in a phase where he was saying "There is nothing you can do." That message was perfect for me at the time, and I knew it, but I did wonder if it was the right message for a lot of the other people.

So my answer is, I suppose, a variation. Instead of thinking of this process where we uncover the truth of ourselves as an action, think of it differently, reframe it as a creative adventure, as a fine art.

Art is only possible because there is extraordinary sensitivity. There is extremely sensitive listening, sensitive looking, sensitive feeling, sensitive living. So become very sensitive to everything that you are doing, thinking, feeling.

For example, for a period of time I kept a journal where I wrote down all my thoughts at they occurred for a period of 15 minutes to half an hour. I did that every day for months.

In terms of this conversation, I would say turn your vision back on to yourself. Can you feel yourself? Where are you? How big are you?

What color are you? Where in the body are you located? Is there an underlying sense of self, of separate existing at all time, or does it go away at times? When I have a peak experience, what happens to my sense of self? Where does it go? How does it come back?

So you are saying ask Ramana's question "Who am I?" but be creative about it. Be a sensitive artist with it. It is not a mechanical thing.

Yes, thank you, that is very good. It all comes from caring, really caring, about yourself. Then you want to be happy, you want to be at peace. You will dig and dig until you find the answer. You sense it is beneath this pile of garbage.

So the "Who am I?" is the shovel to dig through all that you are not. What you are doing is systematically eliminating everything you think and believe you are until you are faced with what you really are. What you really are is not a thought, not an idea, not a concept. When you come face to face with what you really are, there is not enough room for both of you. There is not enough room for the false you and the real you. That's when you realize that the "you" that seemed to be doing all this work was the illusion all along.

It is like a movie with a really good twist. It turns out that the hero is the killer. The detective was seeking the killer and the killer turns out to be himself. He finally wakes up to the fact that it was him all along. Only he knew how to kill without getting caught. So finally he has to catch himself. Then both the detective and the murderer go. They are no longer needed. They have served their purpose. They dissolve into each other. The investigator and the investigated, the yang and the yin, the witness and the ego, gone.

The purpose of life is death. The highest death is the death of the false self. So if the detective in you can find the false self and see it clearly, then it will be like a dark room. The darkness disappears when you turn the light on. The light comes on and everything that was false goes. Even the detective goes. He was needed in the darkness, but in the light he has no role. When there is only light, there are no shadows. There is no I-thought.

Thank you. Now I have a new appreciation of the "Who am I?" meditation.

That's good. That's all that going on anyway. The whole world is going "Who am I? Who am I?" That's the sound of the wind, the water, the world as it spins. That is the meaning of OM. Ommmmm. OM is "Who Ammmmm I?"

But because the way of the world is to look outside, it misses. So you look within. With a little luck and a lot of hard work — or maybe not — you will realize that there is no within. Or the within and the without are one and the same. "I am that" means it is all "I" only.

When you can't find yourself anymore, that's when you find the world as it really is. Until then, you think you are looking at the world, but all you're doing is looking at your thoughts about what you think is the world. The real kicker is discovering that there is no world. There is only YOU. You, the "I," are the Self. The world appears as a lucid emanation of you, as part of you. No world. Only Self. That's the end of the road and the beginning of eternal life in God. In God's world, there is only perfection, only love.

Who Do You Think You Are?

Most people are convinced that they have a mind. They believe they need a mind in order to function in the world. The expression "He lost his mind" describes an undesirable state where the ability to function in the world has been severely impaired.

Then when the idea of "no mind" is presented, it does not make much sense to people. The confusion arises because "no mind" does not mean no thoughts. The error is in believing that you need a mind, an organized structured mind with a control center, in order to have thoughts.

Everyday functioning makes use of thoughts. But the arising of thoughts does not require a mind. Thoughts arise naturally from the Self, from the Heart, from pure awareness. The I-thought is based on the "I am the body" idea. This is the basis for the so-called mind.

You can have thoughts without a mind. You can function perfectly fine without a mind. You can have all the thoughts you need in order to live and not have a mind of any kind. There are thoughts, but no thinker. There is experience, but no experiencer.

The mind is an illusion. Like clouds in the sky, there are thoughts but there is no mind. There is no mind apart from the I-thought. When the I-thought goes, the mind goes.

Who do you think you are?

I don't know. I don't think.

But you have thoughts.

Yes, I have thoughts. Thoughts arise. But I don't think.

Okay, I'm not sure what that means. So who are you?

I am whoever or whatever you really are. I am the peace and happiness that surpasses understanding.

To just understand, to just know, that sucks. It is not enough. It is the booby prize. You must transcend understanding and thinking. The thinker must die. Then thoughts come and go, but they are just the wind blowing. They are clouds floating in an empty sky.

The world process requires thoughts, it requires facts, it requires details. So and so did such and such at here and there. It is all about the senses, and it is all nonsense.

How do I do Self-inquiry?

That's a good question, but the real question is "How can I get Self-inquiry to do me?" The illusion at the beginning, and even for some time, is that "you" are "doing" self-inquiry, or "Self-inquiry" with a capital S.

But there is not inquiring into the Self with a capital S. There is no going into or out of the Self. What is really taking place is that the Self with a capital S is inquiring into the nature, the reality, of the tiny false little self that bases its existence upon the temporary fragile soon to be dead physical body.

If the Self with a capital S was not behind all of this inquiry stuff, then none of it would work. Maybe a better word picture is that the big Self is slowly but surely dissolving the small self. It will happen sooner or later, after hundreds of lifetimes. Eventually, the big Self wears down the small self to nothing.

But what do I do?

Go into the self-inquiry with total earnestness. Give it all you've got. Then at some point the big Self takes it over. That's when you realize that if you "try" to do self-inquiry, you are actually getting in the way. So then you can let go and trust. You drop the mental inquiry and the process goes on wordlessly.

But like priming a pump, you must get it going. What I am talking about is probably classified as the "advanced" stage.

But it makes perfect sense. What you really are cannot be described in words. If it could be, then you would be in the dictionary, and that would be the end of you. Death by dictionary.

What I meant is how do I do the technique, the step by step?

The main point is the discovery that the I-sense, the I-feeling, is not based on the physical body. This is what everybody seems to believe and they act on this, but when this assumption is closely examined, it is found to not be true.

The experience of "I" arises independently of the body. So asking "Who am I?" is an investigation into the FEELING of I. What would it matter what you think?

When you were little, you played with toy soldiers. Now you are a policeman. Later you get married and you become a father. Your roles keep changing, your thoughts keep changing, but there is an experience of continuity.

This experience of continuity is what you are examining. We are not Buddhists, so we are not going to look for a "no-self." Instead, we ask "What is the true support, the steady reality behind this apparent continuity?

You body has changed. Your life has changed. Your career has changed. Your relationships have changed. Yet you have not gone crazy because through it all there has been this more or less unbroken continuous sense of self.

The lazy habit of people is to attribute this unbroken continuous sense of self to the body. Because the body has continued, more or less, they think that is the basis for their feeling of a solid unchanging self. This is what the parents, society, celebrities, teachers, everybody is telling them. So it must be true, right?

People are lazy and they don't look. When finally you do look, then you find that the body is transitory. The body cannot be a solid foundation.

You must discover it directly for yourself. The body is constantly changing. See it yourself. Physics tells us this. The physicists know the truth, but only intellectually. They don't live it.

So when you ask "Who am I?" it is not a thought question. It is a feeling question. You move beyond the thought, the phrase. That is just a teaching tool, so everybody can talk about "Who am I?"

When you actually do it, what you do is intimately study the FEELING of me, of this I. As it arises in the morning at the instant you wake up. As it fades away as you go to sleep. And throughout the day. What is this feeling of being? Is it really based on the body? If the body is constantly changing, can it really be so?

If you like, do the two-step meditation and challenge each and every arising thought. "Who are you?" followed by "Where did you come from?" or some variation of that.

So it's not really "Who am I?" but "What is the feeling of I?"

It is personal. Everybody does it a little differently. It is like music or painting. You develop your own style. But you must master the basics first. It is not analysis. It is the art of intuitive investigation.

The key is to recognize that the error comes from thinking "I am the body, I am so and so." You are fine when you say "I am." So you shift from "I am the body, I am so and so" to "I am."

Ramana advised repeating "I-I." This helps some people to stay focused on the I-thought and not get lost in their stories and the world. If you just say "I am" and stick with that, you experience a pure feeling. Go ahead. Try it.

I am. I-I-I ammmm. I-ammm. Yeah, okay. If I just say "I" I feel it up in the head. But if I say "I amm" then it's like I'm opening a little door into being, into just being.

Very good. "Um, am, yum," these are sounds of the heart. I would say work with that some more. Make it a meditation.

This stuff is very personal. That's why I'm in favor of people trying many techniques until something sticks. But once a person finds something like that, something that works for them and speaks to them, then they should dedicate themselves to it and go all out with it. Their search phase is over. Now they need to go all out in their application of this personalized spiritual method. To find it was Grace itself.

When you go from "I am" to "I am so-and-so," you get stuck in the world with super-glue. That's the outward direction, into the world. You totally reverse the direction and go from "I am the body who is so-and-so in the world" to just "I am."

But then eventually even "I am" is too much. The "am" is like OM. It is the sound of creation, so it subtly tends to go outwards. So you drop the "am." Then you are left with "I." Then there is only "I." It turns out that this "I" is universal. It is everything.

Since we're playing with sounds, the sound would be like the wind. So it's not "I" like an announcement "I am here." It is more like a sigh, a subtle sigh of the invisible wind: I-I-I... I-I-I... I-I-I....

You dwell intimately in the pure untouched open center of the "I" feeling. You abide in the core of any sense of localization that is left. Eventually even the feeling of "I" of any kind is found to be a burden, a limitation. When you see this, then it drops off by itself. Then there is no "I" at all. Then oneness goes, too. There is no perceiver of oneness.

This state of "no I" is neither the presence of some kind of "I" nor the absence of an "I." So it is not a "blank," it is not a something. It is not even the absence of the absence of a something. This openness is understood to be the real "I," the pure universal "I." It is wide open and perfect like the big blue sky. Eventually it is seen that even the world is just this universal "I." There is only this universal "I." It is the "I-I" or true identity.

But being vast emptiness sounds like a big void. That hardly seems like something worth having or experiencing.

It sounds like that because the notion of your precious small self not existing sounds like the ultimate disaster that could happen to you. Frankly, it is. "Life with me. Me all day long. Me me me." That is music to the ears of the ego. Yes, yes, yes... me me me.

Life without me? That's incomprehensible to most people. Terrifying. But in fact this "me" is the real problem. It is why the world suffers so much. The ocean of suffering begins with that little devil, the little separate me that is identified with the body.

As for steps, just start by closing your eyes. Be on the lookout for the mind to say that the feeling of "I," of existing, of being, comes from the body. Listen to this, then let it go.

Keep digging with your feeling for where this feeling of "I," of being, of existing, of presence, of aliveness is really coming from. Keep letting go of the mind and you will find the feeling of "I" in your heart. I can guarantee you it is not coming from the physical body! That is just an unexamined myth. Upon investigation, it falls apart.

I will try that.

Good. To summarize, you do feeling-sensing within to find out that the sense of "I" is not based on the body. Then you realize it is not limited to the body. This is the pure feeling of "I am." But that is not the end because it is still bounded and it is still changing.

You keep studying and investigating with your feeling sensitivity, with your heart, with the core of your being, and what happens is the "I am," as glorious as it is, it too falls away. It falls away so that the pristine "I," the supreme universal "I," can be revealed.

The pure "I am" is very cool. There is a luminosity to it. It is blissful. It is above the usual state. You will be tempted to stay there awhile, and you probably will. I know I did.

This is where some people get stuck. They think this pure "I am," this golden glow, is "illumination." They think this narcissistic core is the enlightenment, so they get stuck.

The outgoing tendency is still intact. You can get stuck in the ecstasy of the feeling of "I am." It is a delicious feeling. It feels good. To be "I am" is still tending to become "I am so and so" in the world. It is a trap.

"I am" is a dangerous place to linger, but I think typically people often do linger there, if for no other reason than it is so beautiful. It is beautiful, but the world is not destroyed. If there is a world, you will get drawn back to it. That is why I say "There is only the Self." That means no world. You must keep going until any sense of localized "I" and any sense of difference, even any sense of oneness, is totally gone. Only then is the world gone.

When I was doing Nisargadatta's meditation of dwelling in the "I am" feeling, of resting in the pure feeling of being, I arrived at an experience of the "I am" that was a golden ball of light. I reached a state where inwardly I experienced myself as a beautiful pulsating golden egg floating in space. This was the "I am" which was in love with itself, which loved to be. This was my individualized personalized edition of that Cosmic "I AM" Consciousness.

It was subtly moving, humming, vibrating, pulsating. Little ripples would rhythmically sweep across its surface. It was like it was a living music. It was a beautiful golden ball of light that was humming and singing to itself. It felt very good. It was sweet, almost too sweet, like really good candy that's bad for you.

This golden ball of light of "I am" was very captivating, very alluring, very seductive. Psychologically, it was "sticky." It was like fly paper. When you touched it, you stuck to it. I had never experienced anything like it. It dawned on me that this was the primal ego glue. This was the super-sweet narcissistic intoxicant.

As I listened to what it was humming, I realized it is humming the song of "I love me. I love myself. I love me... me... me... me." It was saying this to itself over and over and over again. It was "me me me me..." without end. It was "all me" all of the time.

If it could speak, here's what this mantra of "me" seemed to be saying. "Oh yummy yum yum. How much I love myself! So much! So much! I am so delicious. Mmm." It wasn't really words. It was a feeling. A feeling of being in love with myself, of adoring myself. But this was not conscious self-love. It was unconscious addiction. It was an obsession. It was self-absorbed, blind, dangerous.

When I meditated on that golden egg and became that golden egg, there was a great peace in it. But coming out of the meditation, exiting from the concentration, it was hard to integrate this peace back into daily life. I continued to do this meditation but I began looking elsewhere. I did not know it at the time, but this dwelling in the pure feeling of "I am," in the self-indulgent rapture of the beautiful golden ego egg, would be a natural bridge into Ramana's "Who am I?" meditation.

This sounds like narcissism, the myth of Narcissus. Narcissus fell in love with himself.

This is the discovery of the fundamental narcissism that is the root problem for us human beings. This is the false core, the false love for the false self. We are worshiping ourselves, we have made ourselves into tiny little upstart gods.

So it can be a real shock to realize that at the core, at the very center of your being, is this undiluted selfishness. But this is not your real center, your spiritual center. This is the center of the false self, of the small self, of the body-based "I."

So when you see this beautiful little ball of light that is pulsating so happily and going so merrily along its way, or whatever you see or experience as "I am," and see it for what it is, then it falls away by itself. This happens because what is seeing this ball of light so clearly is NOT the ball of light! That which can see this false "I" as false is the true "I."

That's when you know the true "I" and you know that you are the true "I" and not the false "I." Make no mistake. Although it is very subtle, the false "I" is the body-based "I."

It must claim a body in order to perpetuate itself. It cannot just claim space. It must have a location, a station, a destination, a vehicle.

At the heart of the I-thought is a localized I-feeling. The heart of the localized I-feeling is the real Heart, the unbounded pure I-feeling. Do not end your investigation until you get there. The localized I-feeling is relatively pure. It will feel like a state of rest. But it is still unstable. Keep investigating until the I-thought itself is seen for what it is and falls away.

Even the experience of oneness, the perception of oneness, is a limitation. You can go through a phase where you look out at the world and you have the feeling "I am all of that. I am one with that. All of that is me. I am that." But that is still a perception of the world as "other" because you are having an experience of it.

You are not done until everything is gone. That includes being one with everything. Cosmic consciousness, the Cosmic "I AM," to be one with the universe, it is not the end. It is another stage.

What is the role of the body in all of this?

Ultimately the body is just along for the ride. Like St. Francis said, it is "brother donkey." It is doing all the work, the universe is working through it, but it is the mind that is screwing with it because the mind thinks it is all that, that it is the big deal. The small "I," the very subtle false "I" that I am pointing to, that is just a thought. That is the seed thought that produces the mind.

Without that central narcissistic I-thought, which is specifically the "I am the body" thought, then there is no mind. There are thoughts, but just like a flock of birds can fly together in elegant formation, that formation is just a temporary coming together for a purpose.

When the purpose is over, then the birds break away from each other and the formation is completely gone as if it never existed. Then there is open space, blue sky, and that was always there.

So the birds come and go, individual birds, formations of birds, but they are just birds, and there is nothing to them except to come and go and do the work of the universe to maintain the functioning and destiny of bodies.

How Will I Know I Have Found My Real "I"?

What is the relevance of this investigation into "Who am I?" The relevance is that you, like any other human being, want to be happy. As long as you think happiness is gained by doing this or having that or being so and so, then you will choose that other possibility over Self-inquiry.

Why is that? Because Self-inquiry is difficult. It is the most difficult thing. It is the most rewarding thing. The best was saved for last. Typically, we try everything else first. After none of that stuff works for us, then it occurs to us to look inside. Then we look inside in all kinds of ways. We think we're doing something new. This is called "the search."

But the search does not yield the answer, either. We were still searching for something, for "it," for the magic bullet. Even though we were looking inside, we were still looking outside of our self, outside of our true self. Finally, we ask the question "Who is it that is doing this seeking, this looking, this questing, in this first place? Who am I?"

That is when the jig is up. The truth comes out. When you find your real "I," then the search ends. It ends itself automatically. The whole momentum disappears. Before, there was a gnawing, a burning, a relentless ache that would not go away. Now that ache is gone. Now you feel at home no matter where you go or what you do. Now you are free.

You say you are me. But you don't know my thoughts. You don't have my feelings.

In the real Self there are no thoughts. Thoughts come and go but there is nothing happening. There is a feeling but it is the pure essence of pure feeling. It is the supreme fragrance of absolute Being. It is the essence of the essence. The minimum download that the body requires from the universe to keep this body functioning with a name to it is maintained. That is all.

So a meeting in thought is neither here nor there. The meeting is in feeling. True feeling is like open space. It is here and everywhere. So we are one in feeling for we are the sublime universal "I" sense. There is no movement. It is beyond moving and not moving. It is quintessential peace.

I am the real you just as you are the real me. We are here having a dialog, but this is just a convenience. The wind blows two things around at the same time, but there is only one wind, and it is invisible except to the wisdom eye.

How will I know when I have found my real "I"?

You will know you have finally found the real "I" because there will no longer be anything missing. You will be stunned by the sheer perfection of everything. You will wonder why you could not see it before. Your seeking will stop completely, bringing you great joy.

Even the shenanigans of Hitler and Stalin, killing millions and millions of people, even these things are perfect. It is all perfectly perfect, and you would not change a thing. You realize that this grand and glorious dream machine must be exactly the way it is. It is brilliant beyond human understanding.

The human mind is like a tiny stinking turd next to it. There is a cosmic super computer running it that is like a billion Einsteins. You cannot touch it. Your body-based intellect arrogantly tries to analyze it in order to conquer it, but all it finds are indecipherable footsteps in a murky mud. It is all quicksand.

Drop the mind even for a moment and you will see the futility of the mind's search for answers and control. The mind turns gold to iron, happiness to sorrow, love to dust. The mind is a magic machine designed for the mass production of nightmares.

The mind looks at the Grand Canyon and all it sees is a big hole. It can't stop thinking about yesterday when somebody said something to somebody, or the body twisted its ankle after tripping on a rock.

The Grand Canyon is not a hole. The Grand Canyon is God. It's God shouting at you "Wake the hell up!"

Why do people have experiences but they don't change? What is the point of the spiritual search if you can go through all this and end up in the same place?

The answer to why you still feel like crap is that to be who you really are is not an experience. Experiences come and go. Experiences require an experiencer. Experiences are all about "me," a sure sign that the narcissistic center is still there.

But when the false center finally drops away, then you cannot distinguish your happiness from the happiness of others. You may even have trouble distinguishing yourself from others, from cats and dogs, from the world.

However, you have to function. So you are in the world and you learn all over again how to be, just like a baby. You don't own this body, but it's on loan to you, like a car. So you learn to drive.

You learn how to get along with everybody who still thinks they are the body. You shake your head in amazement that they don't see, but you learn how to go with it.

Wholeness is happiness. Wholeness is peace. There are no holes in wholeness. This primordial seamless wholeness was never not complete, whole and perfect. It does not know or remember anything other than itself as purely that.

Then you have no more questions. You just enjoy life. There is still pain and pleasure, but there are no real problems anymore.

Sometimes you get what you want. Sometimes you don't get what you want. Who is there to care? Nobody. Without resistance life is good.

It is like you are on permanent vacation. You used to work hard, long days in a factory. But the factory burnt down and now there is nothing left. In its place they put up a park.

The trees have flowers and the birds are singing. You are on retirement, you get a stipend. There is no work for you. There is no factory. At long last, you are totally relaxed. Nothing to do and nobody to do it. However it looks to others, you are doing nothing.

It sure looks like you are doing things to me. You know... like talking?

In fact, things get done anyway. The universe does everything. It works very hard. It is a super machine. Knowing this, I can relax. The big universe takes care of it all. Talking happens. People with questions happen. Everything just happens.

The existential agony that drove all of this seeking from the beginning is gone. It is replaced by the joy of being, by the joy of IS-ing. There is nothing to do, and it is the greatest feeling in the world. It is called "peace" but really, you cannot describe it. There is nothing to do and nobody to do it, but whatever needs to get done still gets done.

Yes, in case you are wondering, it is the best feeling in the world, or out of it, for that matter. It is even beyond bliss and love. It is freedom. You are free to just BE. This is an always feeling. It never goes away. The surface may change moment to moment, but the stillness, the fullness, the joy of pure beingness, it remains.

Imagine that your heart is exploding with love and joy. You feel like your heart is going to burst you are so happy. But then the vibration of that speeds up so much that it becomes a stillness. It is now moving so fast that its movement cannot be detected. So the joy is there, the love is there, but as essence, as expressions of transcendental wholeness.

Freed of their dualistic imprint, feelings become celebrations of serenity. In the music of total silence, they are the permanent echoes of eternity. There is only That, majestic and supreme.

You are more magnificent than you can imagine. The universe itself depends on you. Peace, love, happiness, joy, these feelings are the bank account of infinite pure being. I am That. I am That. I am That. This is the song of the Supreme. It is ultimate.

You have finally come home, and you know it. You are home. Home Sweet Home.

There is a saying "Home is where the heart is."

The saying "Home is where the heart is" has it exactly right. That is where our home is... in the Heart. The Heart is our Home. It is our Self. We are the Heart. There is only the Heart. There is no world. There is only the Heart.

The Heart is the source of love, but it is beyond love. If you are on the path of love, that is a good path. If you are honest with yourself as you love, you will find the true Self.

But love is still between positions. I am in this position and you are in that position and between us the love flows. Even if it is unconditional love, the positions who are doing the loving are still separate.

So when you inquire into the source of love, having arrived at true unconditional love, non-judging love, a love that is for everybody, then you will find that even that perfect pure love falls away. It falls away because it is not its own source.

The source of love is the Self, the pure "I." All is "I." Nothing is not "I." Naturally, I love myself, and in loving myself, I love all. When there is only "I," all problems are resolved. There is only love.

If God Offers You Enlightenment or a Billion Dollars, Take the Billion Dollars

In modern times, money has taken on a superstar role. It has always fascinated human beings. Yet its role is mainly utilitarian. We use it to buy food and clothes, pay our rent or mortgage, go to a show, take a vacation. The bigger appeal is to the ego. That is why millionaires and billionaires will say "Money? There is never enough money."

Unless a person has extravagant tastes, a million dollars a year in income will more than suffice. In that sense, then, six figures and certainly a million a year net after taxes will meet all practical and even pleasure needs. So the missing factor as to why there is simply not enough money for people who crave money has to be the ego.

Paradoxically, for money to give you a real kick, for it to mean anything much at all beyond survival and creature comforts, the ego must be participating in full force. Then a trip to Las Vegas brings multiple rewards. Dapper paid pseudo-servants bow and scrape before your kingly well-heeled presence. Yet without your dollars you are nobody.

Whether the subject is money or something else, for the ego, for the I-thought, there is never enough and there will never be enough. The reason for this state of affairs is that the ego I-thought is itself the very state of lack. It is the embodiment of alienation. It left its home in the Heart and now wanders, crying in the wilderness of its own ignorance. It cannot be satisfied. The biggest favor you can do it is to end its miserable existence.

I will always remember Ramesh Balsekar saying this, to take the million. I was fortunate enough to be at the talk where he said it. Now with inflation and the value of the dollar going down and there being so many millionaires, now it should be a billion dollars.

Million or billion, what difference does it make? Isn't enlightenment supposed to be the supreme experience?

That's the point exactly. It is not an experience. For there to be an experience, there has to be an experiencer. And that's Ramesh's point. When the experiencer drops, what then is the point of having a billion dollars?

Because of your human conditioning, you know what a billion can do for you. But to the sage where the experiencer has dropped, then the billion dollars could just as well be a billion marbles or a billion flowers or a billion pieces of candy.

Believe it or not, it doesn't mean anything. Now if you give an enlightened person a billion dollars, he will probably spent some of it and put the rest in a bank. He might hire financial advisers and lawyers just like any other reasonable person. Looking on the outside, your reaction might be "He is like anybody else. What is this nonsense about him not caring?"

Well, in India, often the sages do act just like that. You give them a stack of money and they burn it in a fire to keep warm. They are making a point. Money is not the Self. But my point is simply that money is not the problem. It is not the solution either. Money is just a part of modern life.

You don't expect the sage to walk around wearing no clothes. In this country he will get arrested. In India, you can walk around naked and some sages do that. Again they are demonstrating "See, it doesn't matter." But in the West, if a sage wears clothes or has money in a bank account, it is not a sign of error. When in Rome, do as the Romans do. In America, make money.

Is that why so many spiritual people have trouble with money?

I had trouble with money for many years. I traced it to several different past lives as a Christian and Buddhist monk where I had taken a Vow of Poverty.

I also found that I had some very violent past lives in which murder and the death of my family and other horrible things had occurred over my greed for money and lust for power. So I had the feeling of traumatic and tragic deaths associated with money deep in my psyche. I had a lot of stuff to work through.

So I worked through that and along with other things, I arrived at being at peace with money and loving money as the Self. Money is the Self. Everything is the Self.

If you say money is the Self, that's like saying money is God.

Yes, money is God. Money is the Self. You are the Self, too. Everything is the Self.

Wait a minute. You just said money is God. Isn't that some kind of heresy? First you tell me that I should take the billion, not enlightenment. Now you tell me to worship money as God.

I'm not really talking about money. God is everything. Everything is God.

Everything? Even the Devil?

I have a silly but enlightening joke I like to play on people. Let's try it.

I say to you "I have the ability to know what the Will of God is at any time. Would you like me to demonstrate it?"

Yeah, sure. What is the Will of God with regard to the Middle East?

That's easy. The Will of God is whatever happens. So whatever is happening in the Middle East right now is exactly what God wants to happen. Anywhere on the planet, whatever happens, it has to be the Will of God. There is only God. There is only the Self. So whatever happens came directly from the Self. It is super simple.

So you are saying that all of the tragic deaths, all the horrible things in life — these horrible things are the Will of God, the work of God?

Yes, exactly.

I am not comfortable with that.

Why should you be comfortable with that? What kind of God is that? Is that a God of love? That is a very strange love that creates people and then kills them off mercilessly in horrible painful ways.

But you are saying all of that is God's will.

Yes.

You are contradicting yourself.

Your reaction comes from believing that you are the physical body. You are emotionally attached to it. You see your impending death in the deaths of others and you cannot bear the sight.

What? You are not the body? You are talking to me right now!

The body is talking to you right now. I am not the body. I am the universal Self.

Fine. Even if you are the universal Self, if I stab you with a knife or shoot you with a gun, you're going to feel pain, right? And if you died as a result of that, are you telling me it honestly makes no difference to you at all?

Remind me to add a full body search to the security at the door! I get what you're saying, but what you are talking about is the extreme, not the norm. When I said that you can drop the belief that you are the body and stop identifying with it, I did not say you lost all contact with it.

This body still operates, but it operates because the universe wants it to operate. Not only that, it operates the way it does at any given moment because that is exactly what the universe wants to be doing with it. When the universe terminates the operation of a body, we call that death.

The body that you see before you, that is talking with you, is a puppet of the universe. That's the practical truth, plain and simple. The term for this condition is non-doership.

When you are functioning in this way, it is obvious to you that God or Nature or the Universe is 100 per cent in charge. You are just along for the ride. Our planet earth is the ultimate amusement park.

That's crazy. You are telling me with a straight face that you are really a robot. Not only that, somewhere in your twisted mind you think that I am going to want to join you in your mindless robot puppet world? Not a chance. I'll take my free will in a universe full of unexplored possibilities with a healthy dose of suffering over that soul killing garbage.

What we humans think of as love is not universal love. It is human love. It is not the definition of love that the universe follows. The definition of love that the universe follows is "I love to be. I love myself so much, I want to be many. I love myself so much, I want to experience myself in myriad infinite ways. I love myself so much, I want to have lots of little me's who think they are their body running around loving each other and loving me. I love myself so much, I want to know what everything everywhere is like. I love myself so much, I want to taste every single experience, beautiful and ugly, blissful and painful, holy and profane. I love myself so much I even want to see what it is like to die and then be reborn as a human being one thousand times." Then, finally, it says that is enough and there is so-called final liberation or enlightenment in a human life.

I am a mother. I have three children. That sounds like the family through generations to me. A man and a woman get together and out of their union there is born a child. This child grows up and has many experiences. She has children. Her children have children and so on. She can have a wonderful life, she can give birth to more children who carry her heritage on, but in the end, she dies, her body dies. That's life. That's the way it is.

Yes, that's the spirit of it. It is bitter sweet. There is no getting off of this merry go round. It just keeps spinning and spinning and spinning. When you've had enough, you start looking for a way out. Eventually, maybe after many lifetimes, you do find the way out.

So then you exit the machine. You are free of the machine, but the merry go round keeps spinning and spinning and spinning.

Even your exit, your place as observer, is all part of the grand process. It is not your place to end it. This merry go round is God's idea. It is not for you to contest it or change it.

So what you are saying is that God is not love, as some say, God is the artistic super-creator. And any creator worth his salt is going to create a masterpiece of light and dark, with both good and evil in it, just like the movies. The hero needs the evil villain.

In his famous book *Autobiography of a Yogi*, Paramahansa Yogananda talks about the "chiaroscuro" of suffering. This is a most interesting word found exclusively in art.

The dictionary definition of "chiaroscuro" is "the use in painting or drawing of high contrast between light and dark (shadow), perhaps to produce a three-dimensional effect." This is very close to what you just said.

I suggest you read from "Chapter 30: The Law of Miracles." The 1946 first edition is apparently in the public domain. It's available on the Internet. (5)

Yogananda sees a newsreel about World War I. Deeply troubled by what he saw, he prays to God for an answer. God replies by saying there has to be light and dark in order to have a movie. That's all this world is. It is just a movie. Who and what you are is beyond this. The pain and suffering here stimulate human beings to remember the true Self.

If the earth was like heaven, filled with peace and joy, there would be no need for God or enlightenment. So the answer is life is like a chiaroscuro drawing or painting. It has to be this way. For there to be a limited creation, a physical creation, it has to be this way.

So he is saying that since death is false, we don't really die? Then it's all good? That still doesn't explain the suffering. The purpose of all this terrible suffering is to whip us into shape and remind us of God's love? That's crap! The people who are suffering in this world are the good people.

The evil people are partying it up! They're pimping out their female slaves, selling drugs, exploiting helpless children. Maybe that chiaroscuro idea works for a famous yogi living in a plush ashram by the sea. I live in the real world!

We are all guilty of trying to control the world. We want the world to be the way we want it. We don't like it the way it is. That is a guarantee of suffering if ever there was one. The world grinds on with or without you. Resistance is futile. It is a recipe for suffering.

I agree that trying to control the world, which obviously you cannot control, is a stupid idea that is bound to stress you out. But you still haven't answered the question. Why is there so much suffering in the world?

The answer is to eliminate the perceiver who sees the world process this way. Basically, instead of looking at the world the way an embodied person does, you want to look at the world the way God looks at the world.

When you look at the world through the mind. you don't see the world at it really is. You see your personal mind stuff. There is a saying "The pickpocket sees only wallets."

The painter looks at his painting and he knows it like nobody else. When you realize your true nature, then the world as such disappears. You see that the world is God's creative process and you let it go. The world, including all of the busy human bodies, is God's activity, not yours.

I'm sorry, but that makes no sense. How can you be beyond the creator?

The world and its creator are not separate from each other. The painter and his painting are not separate from each other. The ultimate God that you are talking about is the Self, but the Self is not involved in the creation. Even the creation, the universe, will eventually get destroyed. But the Self, the ultimate foundation beyond time and space, will not be affected. It lives forever.

Don't look to the God, look to the God beyond the God. God is a concept. Look beyond all of the concepts.

Yes, only in Silence can the real God be discovered. In that Silence, nothing is. There is no universe, no world and no God. They are all just concepts, imagination. When concepts and imagination stop, their creations come to an end.

But all of this relies upon an invisible foundation that rarely gets acknowledged. That foundation is the Self, the pure Ground of Being that is beyond coming and going, creation and destruction, life and death.

The universe depends on the concept of space. The concept of space depends on the concept of time. The concept of time depends on the concept of existence. The concept of existence depends on the concept of a creator.

The concept of a creator, upon which all the rest of the universe with all its levels depends, itself depends upon pure sublime nothingness. This pristine nothingness is not existence. It does not exist in the usual sense. It is beyond existence and non-existence. It is beyond birth and death.

So all I am saying is that I am this pure nothingness and so are you. Not above or below anything. Not the presence or absence of anything. Unfortunately, it cannot be described.

The world comes and goes within it. The world is nothingness inside of nothingness. For this reason, it is said "Nothing has ever happened."

The changing world is an illusion created by God. God totally runs this show. As an expression of the Self, the world is the Self. There is no world apart from the Self. There is only the Self.

Everything can come and go,
Let us all enjoy the show,
What it is we never know,
But we can watch it go go go.

In the end, it's all the same. It's just words, just an explanation. The real answer is to directly know. The only thing that will really make a difference is to intuitively understand from the Heart.

Then you know for yourself and that's that. The world still goes on its merry way, with or without you. You as the Self realize that the world is inside of you, but that does not change it for others.

"Why is there all this suffering?" is not the best question. A better question is "Who is perceiving this suffering? Who is judging this suffering? Who is reacting to this suffering?" Find out who that is and you will have your answer about the suffering, too.

I am talking to you because I want to suffer less. Instead, I have discovered a new way to get a headache. Trust me, I have no interest in becoming nothing. Bliss maybe, like some spiritual teachers say, but not nothing. The ultimate good is to be nothing? No thanks!

You're right. I did not do a very good job of selling it. When your suffering is so intense that you can't stand it, then you become interested in liberation at any cost. It turns out that there are plenty of bonuses — love, joy, peace, bliss.

Probably to me the biggest benefit of being nothing and nowhere is the peace, the stillness, the exquisite feeling of unbounded freedom. You are off the hook. You are free from the grid. You are home free.

Before you were plugged into the universal machine which is always changing, changing, changing, and forcing you to change with it. Now, finally, you are unplugged. For me, that is enough. The sense of release in itself is pure bliss. Nothing needs to be added.

Sounds like nirvana.

It could be. But some people talk like nirvana is one pole of existence, an anchor in stillness, that is connected to an opposite pole of existence, the drama of activity. I don't look at this that way. For me, this includes everything. Everything can continue as before.

My life can be completely normal, nothing special on the outside. But I will be free and I will feel free at all times. I can enjoy everything to the hilt, yet at no time is anything missing. There is only this natural ever-rich overflowing super-fullness.

Life is a river that delights in its own twists and turns. Life is a rainbow of colors ever-changing, a kaleidoscope of endless potentials sparkling in a daring dream. Life is ever new, ever fresh. Like a child, I forget everything so that I can be completely surprised again the next day.

At the risk of sounding like now I'm selling it too hard, every day is Christmas for me. The world is new for me every day. God is born daily for me and in me. The world is reborn as pure divine Light through Him. The present, the only real experience, is a wonderful present, or gift. To play on the words, the present of the now is a precious present for those who are fully present.

Some years ago I had a very bad tooth ache that lasted for days. It really hurt. When I got it pulled out, it was a great relief. You could say that the prolonged pain over a three day period was suffering. You could say that when the tooth got pulled out, that was the end of my suffering.

The distinction for me is that there is no story to it. Yes, the dentist tried to exploit my agony and sell me a $400 root canal instead of a simple extraction for $150. I could make stories out of it. But the pain was pain. It hurt while it lasted, then it was gone. Suffering is making a story out of the pain. Pain is just pain. Pain is temporary.

The word "suffering" comes from a Latin word meaning "to bear." So while pain is pain, it seems to me that suffering is the experience of bearing something over time, of prolonging the temporary impact of the pain into a residual echo effect rippling beyond the point when the pain actually stops. It is thinking that turns pain into suffering.

There is no suffering, as I define it, but there will be pain. Suffering is pain plus thought plus the agony of living in separation from the Self or Source. I have heard it put "Pain is inevitable, suffering is optional." Suffering is reduced by reducing thought, by going on a thought diet. The ultimate thought diet is elimination of the I-thought.

Suffering is eliminated when you eliminate the master thought behind all the other thoughts, the body-identification thought. The suffering is for the separate one. Why does the separate one think he or she is separate? It is simple. They feel separate because they think they are the physical body. They are convinced that the physical body is the source of their identity. The ego I-thought is the "I am the body" thought. It is a trance state.

When the separate one and his or her story is gone, there is still pain because the physical body continues in a physical universe. But there is nobody to prolong thought in reaction to pain to produce what I call suffering.

You are the universe. When you see it clearly, when you finally break out of the prison imposed upon you by your thoughts, it is impossible to be anything else. If you are the universe, you are the author of life itself.

Still sounds like nirvana to me.

If you say so. The price of admission is only everything that you think you are.

Enlightenment Is for Royal Fools

The enlightened person is God's fool. Knowledge is a trap. It is fine for solving physical problems, but it is next to useless for solving metaphysical problems. You cannot think your way out of a paper bag and you cannot think your way out of suffering.

The way out is the close examination of everything you think you know. You must examine the most fundamental assumptions that you are making. For example, "I am a body. There is a world. I am so and so. I get up in the morning and go to work. I am a mother with two children. I am black. I am white. I am brown. I am a human being."

None of these ideas are really true. They are only relatively true. When something is absolutely true it is not subject to change. Anything that is subject to change is only relatively true. It is not absolutely true. Using that standard, what is true?

Knowledge is based on the perception of subject and object. But what is the ground, the space, the field in which subject and object exist and have their interplay?

When you look at a tree, the tree looks back at you. Everything is Consciousness. Everything is God. There is only God. There is only the Self. There is only the one supreme universal "I." Paradoxically, it does not know itself. That is why it is free.

Where does the fool's part come in? You have said enlightenment is for fools.

The fool's part comes in because I have no interest in having a bunch of intellectual enlightenment theorists asking me questions that are better answered by doing a few months of earnest Self-inquiry meditation. It is absurd to think that spiritual effort and hard work are not needed. These armchair realizers are fools.

One of my teachers, the master occultist Al G. Manning, talked about the value of being a fool. Years ago I went to his classes in Hollywood, California.

Al is a gifted spiritual teacher, kind of a Western Zen master. With him everything is light and fun and playful, which is a pretty cool state to be in. He is a genius. Every week I would see him in class and he always had that lightness of being around him. So I have a deep respect for him.

Anyway, one of his themes was "the power of positive stupidity." When I first heard that, I couldn't make heads or tails of it, which of course delighted him to no end. What he meant, or at least my interpretation of it, is that people over-think things to the point of defeating themselves. They out-think themselves. The power of positive stupidity is the ability to NOT know that something cannot be done.

For example, realizing the Self is, statistically, a very bad choice for your life. There is very little chance that you can do it. It is not a great "career choice." But if you are operating with the power of positive stupidity, then that is irrelevant. You will not have the "smart" thoughts that say "Hey, this is really difficult. Very few people achieve this."

It's a little like the saying "Ignorance is bliss," but I like this better. Basically, I'm too stupid, too foolish, too mindless to realize that it is next to impossible to achieve enlightenment in this life. So I will just do my practice every day. I will do Self-inquiry and I won't think about it or worry about how long it's going to take. I will just do it.

A lot of enlightenment teachers and other spiritual teachers say that there is nothing you can do. Just give up. If you get it, then you get it. If you don't, then you don't. But you seem to advocate regular meditation and doing spiritual disciplines like Self-inquiry.

Although I see the point they are making, I don't agree. A number of the teachers saying this kind of thing awakened spontaneously. Naturally they think there is nothing to do. They didn't do anything!

Karl Renz makes exactly that point. I listen to the questions his students are asking him and my reaction is "Karl, these people are thinking thinking thinking. They are not doing Self-inquiry. They should be doing Self-inquiry. They're not you."

After you've meditated for awhile, for years maybe, then you're ready for Self-inquiry. It helps to be passionate about it. If you are not passionate about it, then find another spiritual discipline that you are deeply passionate about it. For me, it was a total passion. I was absolutely enthralled by the process of Self-inquiry. I loved it. It was a love affair.

The power of positive stupidity reminds me of some Zen sayings.

The other idea that "enlightenment is for fools" refers to is the teaching of Korean Zen master Seung Sahn. Fantastic Zen master. He is a glowing human jewel, just a great inspiration. He would say "Keep 'only don't know' mind." Well, he was absolutely right. The "only don't know" mind is, of course, a no-mind mind, a "nothing-mind," and that is the mind of enlightenment.

If I say "keep only don't know mind," what I mean is the mind of a wise fool, of a divine idiot. This is the power of positive stupidity. There is low dullness and high dullness. Low dullness is the low IQ type of stupidity. The high stupidity or dullness is the no-mind. It is fixed and unresponsive. It doesn't move. It is a diamond in the rough, but it is a real diamond. It doesn't know, so it is pure.

Even if this instinctive drive to realize the truth does not have all the facets and shine of a perfect diamond, it has the fixed unmoving stillness power of the diamond mind, of the sacred fool's mind. It is the power of positive stupidity that enables a person to meditate and do their enlightenment practice of Self-inquiry day in and day out.

No energy is being lost. All the energy is going into the actual doing. This is the kind of earnest intensity that eventually leads to the spontaneous non-stop Self-inquiry state of meditation that arises just prior to realization. The sadhana is now effortless. The Self has come forward to finish the job. The Self takes over.

The deep feeling inquiry takes over, and everything is getting inquired automatically. This is the deeper spontaneous inquiry that leads to the ultimate destination. The Self itself has taken over. Then the meditator just has to stay with the process until it completes itself on its own.

The fixed no-mind and the flowing no-mind come together. Eventually, they work it out and what results is something else. Again, you can't really describe it as it is fixed and flowing at the same time. Then you can say the birds fly through an open sky and the birds are your thoughts. Whatever the bird is, whatever the thought is, it doesn't matter. You are the wide open sky.

If you try to do stuff once you've reached spontaneity, if you try to meditate or do self-inquiry as an act of will, you can feel how you are actually interfering. Like a clear stream, it flows on its own. You put your stick in there and move it around, it muddies up the water. You try that several times and you go "Whoa! I better stop. If I do the effortful doing I used to do, it will interfere with the non-doing that is now happening which is apparently doing itself."

Now no method has become the method. That is because you have become the method. Now you just naturally live the method. But at the time, you don't see this. You see this later. At the time you are puzzled and perplexed. But you have learned to trust this process, this way of inquiring. You are positively stupid, so you just do it. You go along with the non-doing doing now.

So you see this and then you just sit by the side of the river and let the river flow. You know for a fact that this non-doing, where you let the inquiry work deeper and deeper on its own, is the right way. You trust it. It gains even more momentum. All of this is later on. In the beginning there is plenty of effort, sacrifice, hard work and sheer persistence. There is no such thing as a free lunch.

Don't we all start out being fools? Who is the sacred fool?

Yes, the fool starts out by being full of himself. But at some point he realizes that he is the fullness or fool-ness.

The fool is finally full, but in a good way. The Fool card of the Tarot is both beginning and end.

Eventually, the river flows to the ocean, and the ocean becomes everything, and the everything becomes nothing, and then it becomes utterly indescribable because nobody is there. But it's not an absence or an emptiness, it's the paradoxical supreme super-full fullness. If something is super-full all the time so that when add to it or take away from it you don't see a change, it appears to be nothing but in fact it is super-full of everything and then some.

It's the divine fool's foolish and "fullish" fullness. He is a divine fool because to him a pebble and a diamond are the same thing. But being a divine fool, if he is in a real estate deal, he is a tough negotiator. He will fight for every penny even though he knows that every penny is worthless. Or that everything is divine, therefore no one thing is better or worse than anything else. At the practical level, distinctions arise to support human functioning. So he is a tough negotiator! He is a wise fool and a tough customer.

The whole world is in that super-fullness, or super-foolness, yet the world does not even make an impression. Even the world is but a drop in this ocean. The universe is just a drop in this ocean. You cannot describe it. But it is safe to say it is a super-fullness. It is fullness beyond fullness. It is like a billionaire spending a penny to buy the whole universe. Now he owns the universe, yet he is still a billionaire. One penny.

Full and empty are concepts of the mind. This super-fullness that is the Self is beyond the mind. Consider what the situation would be if the mind never existed. No mind ever. What is that?

So it's not a lighter mind, or fewer thoughts, or a more peaceful mind. It's that whole project called the mind, that whole enterprise, that whole organization, is utterly and absolutely missing and gone. It stops cold. It is dead forever. It is like a rusty old car in a deserted junkyard in the middle of nowhere. Nobody cares about it.

But you are not impaired. You find that you can still have thoughts, because they are a part of the natural functioning of human beings.

But you don't need them. You don't need them to be happy and you don't need them in order to function.

You also don't need to be in some kind of ideal silence. The IS-ness of the Self is a perfect kind of stillness that includes both conventional silence and noise. It is completely prior to and beyond both. Take the "l" out of "world" and you have "word."

That is what the world is — words, words, words and more words. These words are a form of hypnotic trance. They are being repeated over and over as trance inductions. Just watch TV. You will see what I mean. Silence is golden. True silence is not just the absence of words. True silence is the death of words. Then you can use words and not get hypnotized by them.

But you don't need a mind and you don't want a mind, because the mind just gets in the way. Some people debate over whether the mind is dead for an enlightened person or not. What difference does it make? The mind has become useless. The Self takes over the functioning.

Like a devious servant who gets the bright idea of taking over the kingdom and then screws everything up, the mind takes over our lives and our world. The mind does not know how to run this kingdom. It thinks it does, but it does not. Without the Light of the Self, it is just a stupid machine. So it just screws things up. Things get seriously messed up when the slave tries to be the master.

All this changes when you give up the mind. The mind unwinds and disintegrates and finally dissolves. It takes time. It is a process.

Due to its massive momentum, its dense heavy insensitivity, its habitual heartlessness, its colossal confusion, its overarching arrogance, its unconscious clunkiness, this is not an overnight thing. Plus the nervous system and the brain need time to adjust.

When the mind is no longer held together by the body-centered narcissism that is the lying cheating heart of its false center, then all of this nonsense, this chaos, this madness, falls away. Like in the fairy tales, instantly the joyful kingdom is back in all its glory.

How the Sage Experiences the World

People who are into relationships are very concerned about "intimacy," but the word "intimacy" is really about that which is innermost — and that which is "innermost" is our very own Essence or True Self within, the Self of All. The mind and even the I-thought are on the surface. They are not the living core. They are not the true center.

It may sound like a paradox, but the very best way to relate to other people is to go as deeply into yourself as possible in order to arrive at your true center, the Heart. When you relate from this Heart, the fact is that many people will find that it is too much. They will make haste to get away. But for those who stay, the rewards are mutual and great.

The super-intensity of the here-and-now two-in-one reality when two people fearlessly engage with full presence as the Self is the answer to the paradox of human intimacy. Living from the non-dual Heart answers the dilemma of "How can I be in a relationship with somebody else and yet live true to the supreme Self?"

The solution is to stabilize in the realization that there were never two. There was, is and will always be only THE ONE. In this One, in the Self, there is only supreme wholeness and wonderful ever-new all-fullness. The ultimate relationship is not a "relationship" at all but pure unbounded Being set free to fully be itself.

I hope you don't mind such a direct question, but what is your experience of the world?

My answer would be that my experience is the experience of the way things actually are. My experience is that although you and I appear to be having this conversation, this exchange between two people, my experience of it is that there is only one reality here. There is no two at all. There is only "I" here. There is no "you."

I don't care about concepts like Advaita or non-duality. I don't even care about the concept of the Self.

Even though I talk about it a lot, that is because there is no better word that I have found. We can sit here in noble silence, but that is not enough for most people. We need to talk and use words, too.

The world is perceived in a functional sense, but the world is not seen as being real. You could say that the world is "seen through." It is seen but it is seen as being transparent. I can see the Light or the Reality that is behind it, that creates it, that informs it and maintains it. The world is the Light, but somehow the forms can be seen. It is poignant almost to the point of pain how real it is that there is absolutely no difference between us.

When the Self is realized, the biggest challenge is then to learn how to function again because you literally cannot tell that you and the cat or the chair or the other person are distinct elements in this world function. You have to learn the art of differentiation all over again, like a baby.

If it is not as earthshaking as that, if it is just a nice experience of "oneness," then I would guess that whatever the enlightenment experience was, it is not going to stick. Realizing your true Self does not just rock your world. It destroys your world and you with it.

When the Self is realized, there is the knowing that you are done. You have achieved what you set out to achieve. At that point, you may commit suicide. I thought about it.

After all, to the Self even the smashing together of galaxies filled with millions of stars is a neutral event, so what to think of this tiny fragile little temporary human body? Just discard it and drop it. Why not?

But obviously you did not drop the body.

No, I did not. I thought of the many people who love me, who care about me. I thought of how they would feel, what they would think. I knew they would not understand.

I also thought of the people I might be able to help someday. So I stayed here. I didn't want to cause people who were close to me the emotional pain and I thought that maybe I might be able to do some good someday, perhaps help others realize the Self.

I would really like you to talk more about your experience of the world.

Take the statement "There is no world. There is only the Self." What does that mean?

I don't know. That's why I'm asking you.

What do you think it means?

That's not fair!

Nobody said I am fair. I am not fair at all.

The experience of the Self is not an experience that comes and goes. If it was something that you had to hang on to as an effort, if it was some kind of special oneness experience, then it would be impossible for it to remain stable at all times.

So anytime anybody is telling you to do this or that and you will be in the Self, you know it's baloney. Realizing the Self is a fundamental change at the level of perception.

It means that you literally see the world in a totally different way. Just as right now it takes you no effort at all to see the world the way you do and to be "yourself," so it takes no effort at all to see the world as the Self, to be the Self.

Is this where the non-doership comes in?

There is no effort to maintain the true state. It is Sahaja — natural and effortless. There is nobody to do the maintaining. That is why non-doership is the critical marker.

No person is qualified to teach Advaita or non-duality unless they are established in non-doership. Maybe they are a scholar, which is fine, but they should say they are just a scholar.

After the advent of non-doership everything changes. This change is impossible to describe. Nor is it the end. But until that stage, there is nothing to talk about. The person cannot possibly know what they are talking about. They are just guessing. They may have some pretty good guesses, but they are not qualified as an authority.

So when I say "You see the World as the Self," that is not a metaphor. You literally see the world AS the Self! So you are seeing, feeling, hearing, being the Self, and you can see the world, but it is like the world is there and not there at the same time like a hologram.

There is a functional representation of the world that can be recognized and responded to, but it is intuitively understood that it is just a holographic representation of the Self, not different from the Self. Something takes place as the Self that is within the Self and does not limit it in any way at all.

That is why talk of "oneness" and "unity" can be misleading. It is beyond oneness or unity. These terms imply the resolution of a duality. The notion of duality depends on the idea of a real world. Duality comes from the idea of somebody who is being a physical body, who is living in a physical world, who is separate from it and looking at it.

But the experience of the Self as the world and the world as the Self is much simpler than that. There is only the Self! No world at all!

It is like your best friend goes shopping and later visits you wearing new clothes you have never seen. In spite of their brand new clothes, you have no trouble knowing it is them. Likewise, the "world" is the Self wearing clothes. It is obvious that it is the Self. It is obvious that the Self is the Self. The clothes are just an adornment. This metaphor breaks down, though, because the world IS the Self. No separation. There is only the Self.

There is no separation to heal. There is no memory of a separation to heal. Since there was never anything other than this seamless absolute wholeness, then unity and oneness are irrelevant. They mean something only in relation to duality, to some kind of split.

Spirituality teaches that the world is an illusion. So are you saying it is and is not an illusion? How can that be?

Yes, for this reason, because it is a projection of the Self, the world is compared to an illusion or hallucination or mirage. But from that, people got the idea that if the world is just an illusion, then to be spiritual I should escape from the world or ignore it or deny it. On the other end of that duality, I can degrade or punish my physical body.

But all of that is nonsense. The realization of the Self is a positive thing. It is a return to the natural Eden of pure innately joyful perception. To live as the Self is to live naturally.

In other words, we should be thinking in terms of an innocence of perception, a purification of perception. We see "through a lens darkly." We need to "cleanse the lens of perception." Living in the Self is the full and final "cleansing of the lens."

An analogy would be that living in the Self, being the Self, is like being an innocent baby who has not figured out the world, who has no idea what the world is, who does not relate to the world as a world. This baby does not have the concept "world."

This baby does not care about money or sex or fame or acclaim or status or clothes or cars or books or Advaita because it has no equivalents for these things. They are meaningless. If there is no world to begin with, then what meaning can they have?

At the same time, this unusual baby can function in the world and do business over the phone and show up for appointments on time. This special yet completely pure and innocent baby can have the lifestyle of a millionaire or live in a cardboard box in an alley or be in front of millions on TV or never be known and die without anybody ever knowing that he realized the Self.

So it is a paradox: a totally functional adult baby. This is the "no mind" baby, the adult "no thought" functional baby in the world.

The world is just a concept. It is just an arrangement of thoughts. This is actually pretty easy to see when you look at the latest events, the latest celebrity, the latest news. It is all based on what people are thinking. If people stopped thinking and stopped buying into the thinking of others, the world would pretty much stop dead in its tracks. The thought virus would die. Remove the thoughts and there is nothing left.

The world is a bunch of thoughts, it is layer upon layer of thoughts, but it has to be maintained daily. If it was not, it would all disappear. Civilization would disappear, technology would disappear. All of that is just thoughts, just thought patterns and habits.

We would be back to being naked more or less living off the fruits of the earth. Life would be very simple. Personally, I think that would be better. But it is not up to me.

Ramaji, you didn't answer my question about how you experience the world!

Sorry. Thanks for holding me accountable. Let me give it another go. Okay, I am looking at you now. Go ahead.

Okay, Ramaji, tell me what you see.

I see your body. I see the other people. I see the room.

Is that it?

I'm not done. Yes, I see those things, but at the same time, I am having the experience that it is all my Self. You are my Self. There is no me here and you there. There is only "I." All of this is my very own Self. All of it, the room included, is my "I."

Is this an experience of oneness?

I would not use that word. Oneness implies the memory of a lack of oneness or a comparison with some kind of lack of oneness. I would say that if you had lived in oneness for so long that no other people and no signals from society reminded you of anything else, so that "oneness" was no longer oneness but that it was the total absence of any person, any notion of a self or a separation, then maybe you could say oneness. It is positive. It is an affirmation. It is a spontaneous embracing of all of the so-called "experience" of you, I, them, the world. It is total. It is life itself, life as it really is.

It is the joyful song of Self. It is the joy of existence. It is not remedial. It is not a fixing of flaws, a filling of holes. There are no breaks in the dam. There is just the one holy wholeness. It was always this way. It will always be this way. There is only one "I," only one Identity, only one supreme Self. That is the way it has been always and forever.

If that is what you mean by oneness, then you could call it oneness. But don't think in terms of an experience of oneness because that implies an experiencer of the oneness.

Now you have a subtle duality, the experiencer as the subject and this oneness as the object. An experience of oneness like that is legitimate as far as it goes, but it is a step or a stage. The apparent experiencer must go. Then the true "I," the universal "I," comes forward.

So you are talking to me and having a dialog with me just like we are two people sitting in a coffee shop, but what you are actually experiencing is that you are a single universal Identity that so totally includes both you and me that there is no you and me. There is a feeling of a Universal I-ness that enjoys total fulfillment because nothing is missing.

Yes. The notion of an "other" creates the pseudo-experience of lack. The authentic fullness is able to play at being two people here without imposing any limitation on itself, any sense of another.

To put it bluntly, I could not find you even if I tried to look for you. You are nowhere to be found. You do not exist. There is only this one "I." To you, you are real, but you are only a concept. But this is not a negation. The universal feeling obliterates all differences.

The feeling "I am this body" is where the false division takes hold. Then I am here and you are there. But this "you" can be subtle, it can even be an experience of oneness. The feeling that goes with being the Self is beyond even "I am all of this." I went through that and "There is only the Self" is beyond that. When you experience that you are "all of this" the "this" is still the world continuing to exist like a vague mist. There is still a subtle gap.

The Self where you can say "There is only the Self" is pure unbounded being and universal I-ness that exists supremely with or without people or world or even a universe. They are all just adornments to the Self. Everything is the universal I-feeling. That is really all that there is. That is the final truth. It could be called Shiva Consciousness.

There is functional differentiation but not essential differentiation. No real difference is being experienced because the body concept is not in the way to create a phony wall or barrier. The Self is HERE NOW for and as all of us, but the body-idea blinds people.

This all sounds so abstract and impersonal. I could say that the Self – the true "I" that we are – IS. It just IS, and it is EVERYWHERE all of the time. That would be true.

But I am going to be poetic for a moment and say something to you that applies equally to everyone in this room and, for that matter, to every single person on this planet: "You are my very own precious beloved Self!" I mean this quite literally!

That is beautiful. That's as good as words can do, I suppose.

It's as good as I can do. If I say to you, "I hate to break the news to you but you don't exist," it would be only half true. Ultimately, it would not be true at all. In fact, you do exist – as the Self!

That is the real source of your feeling of identity, of your feeling of existing. You exist absolutely as the supreme Self. You always did and you always will.

So it is a positive identification. The separate individual body-based little I's have their source in the one true universal "I." Whatever reality these little body-me's, these tiny mini-me's, are felt to have is being siphoned off from the Self with its blessing.

It is like having a wealthy neighbor next door who has a ton of electrical power coming into his house. You secretly use an electrical line to tap into his power and you have all of your services, your TV, your refrigerator and so on. He doesn't even miss it.

But never for a moment was this your power. It was always the power of your rich neighbor. You can piggyback on the Identity power of the Self and take credit for it. This is what the "I am the body" thought does.

But it will always be true that without the Self there would be no Identity feeling at all. The body-based experience is watered down. It is a confined and limiting trial version of the real thing. It is a cheap lousy knockoff.

What Does Love Have To Do With It?

Relationships are a constant if subtle area of confusion in contemporary Advaita and non-duality. For many, relationships (and sex) indicate the call of the world. The temporary resolution of the split of twoness in a peak moment of positive emotion is taken as the sign of success. In fact, there is no success or failure. Relationships are a function of the Divine Will (or functioning of Nature, if you prefer) just like everything else in our lives.

Although surrender can and should be practiced in an intimate relationship, there is very little instruction about it. Until the day comes that Tantric practices become public knowledge and get absorbed into Advaita, the art of regarding your partner as an emanation or expression of Shiva (God) or Shakti (Goddess) will have to do.

What it all boils down to, though, is something that does not require Tantra or any other kind of esoteric knowledge. What it takes is courage. It takes courage to love, and it takes total courage to love totally and all the way. The sad reality is that most of us today do not love all the way. We settle for pathetic substitutes and pay for weak vicarious experiences, then wonder why our shallow existence is meaningless and empty.

Life does not supply the substance, we do. The ultimate "food" is the Heart itself, and it solves all relationship dilemmas and confusion. When you are in a cosmic love relationship, you don't have to think about it. The "other" person quite literally IS "you."

When you are in a relationship that you are living from the Heart, the reality is that it does not feel like you are in a relationship. All you are doing is just being yourself.

A relationship is a concept. There is nothing to figure out. There are no problems to solve. Everything just unfolds, yet nothing really happens. There is no relationship. The dilemma is resolved at the root. The relationship becomes a "realization-ship." There is the unbroken seamless flavor of Reality in all of its splendor and spontaneity.

Every moment of action and interaction is rich and satisfying in itself. In the wisdom of the ever-full and always complete Self, each moment takes cares of itself. You know exactly what to do each moment because "they" are "you." You will know what to do in the moment itself when the moment comes. You do not know ahead of time. There is nothing to figure out. There is nothing to know. Just BE. The rest takes care of itself.

I was in love with somebody and she broke my heart. It was only after that happened that I got interested in enlightenment. Before then, I just wanted to have a good time. What is the role of love in our spiritual growth. How does it help us on the spiritual path?

Maybe you could narrow your question down a bit? That's like asking "What is love?"

Before I got involved with Jennifer, I thought I knew what love was. Then after she broke my heart, it was almost like she did me a favor. My concept of love exploded. It expanded. I realized that I was narrowly focused. Love wasn't just marriage and kids. I realized that love was bigger than that. It is the whole world.

That is very cool. But what is your question?

I guess my insight created new questions for me. Like now I do things where I volunteer to help the homeless, things like that. I feel I am giving love out. But I feel like I am a stranger in a strange land. Am I so unusual that I care?

Most people don't get to where you're at. When they get their heart broken, and most people do sooner or later, and it may be more than once, the tendency is to contract, to curl up and build your defenses like a turtle. Then the older you get, the more hard and contracted and defended you are. You shut down and you are only half alive.

But your response was to allow your broken heart to stay broken in the sense that it had been broken open, and you allowed it to stay open. As you know, there is a special joy to that openness. Once it is discovered, nobody can take it from you.

However, as you are hinting, it is just a stage in the journey to the Self. Not that it is so linear, but in studying the lives of those who realized the Self, it becomes clear that usually there are revelations as to the true nature of love. Realizing the nature of love very often comes before realizing the true nature of the Self, of your natural authentic transcendental Identity. To know the true "I" that you really are, first know love.

Conventional love is a ritual to secure desired experiences, things, advantages. It is self centered, self serving. You scratch my back and I'll scratch yours. You are just using each other. The donations that people make to charity are usually a way to get attention. To find real love, you have to leave the ego far behind. You have to turn to God.

The real love, the pure love, is very rare. In a beautiful married couple who have a true love for each other, you will see something like it. But their special connection is with each other, not with the world. If you take the notion of a special wide open connection with one other person, and then ask "What if I felt this way about everybody, what would that be like?" then you take a step closer to the experience of love as your very own Self.

To be the Self, for everybody to be your Self, can be very painful. I went through years where I was tortured by all the terrible things going on in the world. Or it could be what was taking place in the emotions and energies of the person sitting next to me on the bus. I would feel their stuff as if it was happening to me. This work is only for the strong. Love is not for the weak! Real love is for heroes and heroines. It takes "true grit."

On the flip side, I also went through a phase where everything I saw in the world was incredibly funny to me. I was laughing all of the time. The whole world was just one big non-stop comedy show. I couldn't understand why people didn't see it. They were so freaking serious about it all. At first I thought they were just kidding. But eventually I realized they were deadly serious about all the problems they thought they had.

My problem is that now I feel almost sexless. I feel that my love for others that has this universal quality almost takes over the sex, almost replaces the sexual desire, but not quite. I guess I had expected that being so open and loving would solve all my problems because "Love is the answer." But it isn't turning out that way. I am still subtly conflicted. I still have relationship problems.

I would say that love has answered all your problems and given you a solution to everything, only you do not see it. Maybe you are not ready for that answer yet.

What you are describing is a high spiritual state. Because you are living in the world, you are surrounded by many distractions, not the least of which is women. Ramakrishna, the great devotee of Kali, would repeat "Women and gold! Women and gold! Women and gold!" He had a good point!

I feel very loving but the whole dating thing has gotten weird. I'm not a saint. I work an office job. Yet women find me even more attractive than before. When I go on a date I can feel them wanting to possess me. The sexual attraction is for the purpose of capturing me and owning me. They want me to take my cosmic love and squeeze it down into a little box, tie it up in a little box for them.

What you are talking about is one of the unadvertised secret mysteries of advanced spirituality. I have lost track of how many men I have known who have landed in your boat. They have all told me something very similar. On the surface, it is very strange.

Once they got very spiritual, and I mean spiritual by my standards – it's pretty easy for me to tell what level somebody is at – after they got really spiritual and filled with love, women were attracted to them like bees to honey. And at the same time, in a massive paradox, they found that they did not want to get involved, that they were even scared, frightened of the idea of getting seriously involved with a woman. Suddenly they were a "chick magnet" and they didn't want anything to do with attracting women.

This one guy in Oregon, he was already a very good looking guy. He looked like the classic "Marlboro Man" ad, a rough and ready handsome cowboy type. He started having the most gorgeous women in town hitting on him.

He would be on a bus and one of them would come up to him and slip a piece of paper with their phone number on it into his coat pocket. They would give him a wink, blow a kiss as they did this. It drove him crazy! He didn't know what to do.

I guess I'm kind of in the same spot. What did you tell him to do?

I told him to go ahead and take the date. Go out with her. Go to bed with her. If she was rich, marry her! He wouldn't have to work anymore. Plenty of time to meditate!

I'm only half kidding. All of these guys I have known over the years, these spiritual guys, once their spirituality got to a certain place they found it impossible to commit to a relationship with a woman – or with a man, for that matter.

The reasons they gave were different, but they all amounted to the same thing. One guy was afraid that he would lose all of his spirituality, that the woman with her involvement in appearances, in materiality, would drag him down. Another was convinced that he would lose his spiritual force when he ejaculated. He was convinced that his spiritual life would go down the tubes if he had a conventional male orgasm while making love to a woman.

Yet another simply felt that women added a chaotic level of complexity that he did not need. His point was that they were very distracting. If nothing else, they just plain talked too much. He craved silence. He needed to live simply in order to be spiritual.

This guy told me "I have yet to meet a woman who said to me 'I'd rather meditate than go out to dinner or go dancing. I'd rather meditate than buy shoes or have you present me with an expensive surprise gift. I'd rather sit here in silence with you.'"

What he was missing and what all these guys were missing is the fact that these reasons and many other reasons like them are exactly why you do want to be in a relationship!

There is no greater challenge. If you can master relationships, then you can master life. They are difficult but very rewarding. Some excellent spiritual teacher, I forget who, said something like "Relationships are for the spiritually advanced."

He is absolutely right. Almost everybody is having them, though. It seems we are compelled to have them, most of us, anyway. People I have met who are not in one are usually scared or stuck. A very few are Self-realized. Monks, nuns and priest get special rewards for staying celibate. I think that is pretty strange.

There are exceptions, such as the gifted artist who is in love with his art. Then women may come and go in his life, but his first love is his art. I went through that as a writer. Writing was my first love. Women were second. Ultimately, though, this is narcissism.

Artists are narcissistic. If they are honest, they will admit to it, even celebrate it. Art is a unique and special path. When it is one-pointed towards the transcendental, it can become a spiritual path.

What my friends were pointing to via their experiences was the fact that they had become conscious of the problems that accompany intimate relationships. They had become aware of these problems, and their reaction was then to exclude relationships. They were in a state of push-pull, as they had no interest in celibacy or being a monk. They were out in the world, exposed to all these influences. What to do?

However, for me as a natural tantric bhakta, an erotic sensual devotional type, it was just the opposite. For me, relationships were a big part of my yoga. They were my meditation. So my meditation was that the woman is the goddess. She is the Divine Mother. This enabled me to use my relationships as spiritual fodder, as grist for the mill.

That projection worked for a long time in my life. But eventually it fell apart, and rightly so. But it was very helpful to me for a very long time. Everything is the play, the lila, of the Divine Mother. This is not just a concept. It is the reality.

In 1982 at a Kali Temple in Los Angeles, Mother Kali entered my life and took over. So in my case Divine Mother was setting me up on dates, putting me in relationships, breaking them up as well. I would say that this is true for everybody, they just don't know it.

The other thing that these men were not seeing, and this applied to all of them whatever their natural style of spirituality, is that they were confessing that their meditation, their spiritual practice, their sadhana was weak. In short, they were still quite weak.

Their practice was not yet strong, not manly, not powerful, not Shiva-like in the sense of the Shiva Lingam, the big stone sacred phallus. One of the meanings of the Shiva Lingam as a symbol for the Self is that the clarity, the focus, the consistency, the force of the person's sadhana, their spiritual practice, needs to literally be as "solid as a rock."

There are no breaks, no cracks in Shiva's practice. It is solid all the way through. Lord Shiva's practice is rock hard, rock solid, rock tough. The right attitude is to go all the way all of the time, as if your life depends on it. In this spirit, you end up looking for and seeking out new challenges. You want new difficulties in order to test yourself and strengthen yourself. Playing it safe is not only boring, it is not a respectable option.

So if you want to live dangerously as a spiritual man, get with a woman! In all honesty, they are the best spiritual test there is. Each woman is Divine Mother. The women in your life are Divine Mother. They are there for good reasons. They are perfectly synchronized with you, your life and your spiritual direction.

Just as the Divine Mother gave you birth, the Divine Mother watches over you during your life. You cannot escape Her. Sooner or later, you must face Her. The way that you face Her, at least in the Western world, is through the women in your life.

The problems that these genuinely spiritual men in our American culture are having are due mainly to four things. First, the fact that they have no model to follow. Second, that they are still not sufficiently established in their meditation. Third, that they still do not know what love really is, yet they think they do know and know better than the women in their lives. Fourth, that they do not understand that they have a relationship with Divine Mother via the women in their life. They did not know that She is the Self.

They are still on the path of purification. They have a notion of purity they want to maintain. They are still just preparing. You can only go so far in the monastery. At some point you must come out and test yourself in the world. The woman is the world.

All of these guys wanted to be able to stay in the monastery. They didn't want to have to deal with the world, with the marketplace. But their karma was that they still had to work and live in the world. In doing so, they were meeting women. It was unavoidable. This by itself should be clue enough that there are loose ends, that things need to be worked out and completed. They were stuck in the middle between monk and lover.

If these guys had given up on women, why didn't they just join a monastery?

That's the thing. They had not given up on women. They did not want to be a monk in a monastery. They understood that somehow you have to be your own monastery. You have to be the monastery! If a man gets turned on by a woman, that is natural. That is nature.

But I think these guys thought they could not be natural. Somehow, to be the Self they had to become like air, not human anymore. This is just not true. Not only that, it is impossible. These bodies are run by Mother Nature. She designed them and she made them to be sexual. In the East there are options, but our culture does not offer them yet.

If I try to translate what you just said to my situation, then what you are telling me is that my meditation practice is still too weak? I meditate an hour a day. Isn't that enough?

My answer is yes and no. I think one hour a day every day is a good solid meditation practice. For many years, I kept up a discipline of meditating one to two hours a day. I couldn't always do two hours, so my real commitment was to one solid hour a day. If you have to work, meditating one hour a day is excellent.

What I'm talking about is an issue for the more advanced person, for the person who has had their heart open up and they have kept it open, for the person who meditates and has a solid spiritual practice. They are now a person of knowledge and love, but they are living in a culture of ignorance. This creates a conflict.

In your case, it sounds like you still want to be in a relationship. So I would say that you want to recognize the narcissism, the paranoia of your position. You are wanting to preserve this cosmic love for the world, yet somehow a living breathing human being who is sitting right across from you at the table in a restaurant that you are on a date with is not included in this love for all!

I would say there is definitely a contradiction there. The answer for me, which I believe applies to you, was to be courageous. Face your fears. If you are afraid of the girl tiger, if you feel that the tirelessly hungry dangerous pussycat is going to eat you alive, then let it happen. Face her. Go towards the pussycat! Go into that amazing magnetic black hole!

Embrace the female tiger wholeheartedly! Let the tigress eat you alive! Who cares? She is getting what she wants, right? You're getting what you want, right? You are getting non-duality.

You are getting ego death. You are resolving the split. You are facing the dilemma of how can you love the whole wide world yet not love the woman in front of you. You have resolved it. You are loving her!

Love takes courage. Love takes balls, stones, cajones. You gotta be a man, a real man, to love. Love takes sacrifice. To sacrifice your body is the ultimate sacrifice.

So you sacrifice your body, your life, your mind to Love. You let the Love take you wherever it will. You are the leaf carried on the winds of Love. You are the log carried by the big wild river of Love. You give up your subtle little arrogant game of control.

Don't mistake me. I am not saying become her whiny bitch. I am not saying be just the always nice guy. Love is the greatest force. You are surrendering to Love, not to her.

You let go and you let Love live you. If you are on the path of Love, then this is where you arrive sooner or later. You must give yourself over. You must give yourself up.

In a word, you DIE for Love. This is the only way. To have a meeting with real Love in your life, and then to not go all the way with this real Love, that is to be stuck between two worlds. Behind you is the false phony world of lying and cheating. In front of you is the luminous world of true Love and loving Truth. But you are stuck in the middle. You are the man trying live in the no man's land. When you live there, you get no respect.

You must become strong, strong, strong... and then you choose to die. You sacrifice your body on the altar of Love. The woman is a great vehicle for this. Her gift is to help you dissolve. You dissolve your ego, your sense of separation, your lordship over matter, your cultural superiority over women, in the solvent of woman. Your "guy between the eyes" dies in her eyes, in her mystical eyes.

Great men, strong men, use the opportunity of the ocean-like dissolving power of the female to die. This dissolving power is what the hesitant man fears. But a brave man can "out-female" the female. She is Divine Mother, but usually she is not conscious of it. You surrender consciously to Divine Mother and die in Her.

This woman does not need to be spiritual. All she has to be is a woman. No matter who she is, no matter what her level, she is filled with "nothingness" power. This is a great Tantric secret.

What people don't realize in this culture, a culture which lacks the devotional bhakti yoga and Tantric eros of India, is that the one on one intimate relationship can serve this process very nicely. You can do this process of total surrender in an intimate relationship.

The relationship between love and death is true knowledge. Love taken all the way is death. Death is the way to love. To love is to die. To love all the way is to die all the way.

I think ultimately it's about sex. If I think she is unattractive, I don't feel the same level of conflict. But if she is beautiful, then she stirs up these feelings. I still don't want to give into her. I feel there is a danger. I could get lost in her eyes and never come out again.

Good, good. Yes, that is the feeling. What are you afraid of? Is this not the yoga of romance? Is this not the merging of yin and yang into the super-ultimate, the great Tao?

It feels like a trap, a velvet trap. It's like something gets opened up, but the world won't allow it. Romeo and Juliet, they must die, their love must die. The cold cruel world cannot allow this fire of love.

At one level, that is the way of the world. But don't you find it interesting that the pretty girl disturbs you yet the plain or unattractive girl does not? I think that is a clue.

That is the sex desire, I guess.

More to the point, it is the imagination. The pretty girl is stimulating your imagination more. The plain girl less so. When your imagination is stimulated, your emotions are aroused. When your emotions are aroused, then you have this feeling of conflict. The sex desire is a form of conflict.

You are saying the sex desire is conflict?

Check it out for yourself. When the level of conflict that you are feeling today is high, when you are feeling depressed or hostile or angry or distressed, what is the level of your sex fascination? I think you will find there is a correlation.

But I am not saying that sex desire is itself conflict. I am saying that it is exaggerated, stimulated, blown out of proportion, devalued and overvalued by conflict.

There is a natural state of sexual desire that arises. After all, sex is needed for procreation. But all the rules and laws for sex are missing the point. Sex is a function of Mother Nature. If you do not artificially stimulate it the way we do in this culture, if it is allowed to settle down, then it is just what it is. It is natural. No big deal.

So you are saying it is not really about sex. It is about emotion?

Yes. Sex is emotion in a bottle. That's why people can't handle it. It's not the sex that they can't handle. Sex is just a mechanical act. At the most basic level, it is a reproductive ritual imprinted on our mammalian brains to preserve the race.

What people cannot handle is the emotions that sex brings up as it stimulates the imagination. So if you're ready for it, if you want to learn how to handle those emotions that sex brings up, that relationships bring up, then you welcome that opportunity for spiritual practice. It is emotional healing. It is integration of the heart in real love.

The confusion comes from the widespread misconception that sex is based on the physical body, on an attraction between two physical bodies. This is not true. Sex is an attraction between the two astral bodies. Sexual attraction is energy body chemistry. The emotions are also in the astral or energy body.

We look at a corpse. It is not having emotions. It is not getting turned on by a beautiful woman or handsome man. This sex-emotion energy is in the astral or energy body.

So the spiritual purification through meditation is at some level about purifying the astral body?

Yes, without getting too technical, since I don't think it helps all that much, what we are talking about is the purification of the astral body and of all of the negative emotions, stuck emotions, emotional blocks. There are vortexes in the astral body that need to be resolved, karmic vortexes that contain energy that will continue to influence you until they are resolved.

One way to resolve them, the Tantric way, is to face them directly. Go into a relationship with all three eyes open, with all four eyes open, if possible. Go for broke in this relationship, but maintain maximum awareness at all times and maintain your meditation discipline. Meditate daily. You will feel the need.

Three eyes I get, but not four eyes.

The fourth eye is the open Crown chakra at the top of the head. This is related to surrendering the personal will to the Divine Will. It is not possible until considerable clarity has been achieved via the Third Eye, seeing things as they actually are.

I have to speak up. It sounds to me like you are making women out to be the bad guys. I think that's totally wrong.

It could sound that way, but it would not be true. For one thing, ultimately male or female ends up making little difference. Women I have met who are advanced or are Self-realized are beyond men and relationships. They may be in one or not, but either way, they could not care less. It makes no difference to them.

What I am talking about is the implication that women are trying to trap men and steal their spirituality. That women are trying to trick men so they can have babies.

You could add to that that the spiritual man is still using women, only now for a spiritual purpose. The woman remains an object. The fact is that until you realize the Self, since you think you are the body, then everybody is an object to you. You are a block of wood in a thick world filled with blocks of wood. Everybody is thick and dense. Nobody can be reached, not really.

The only solution is to realize the Self. That is the point. Then you are the open living "I," the soft everywhere "I." Then you are everybody, every person. Then you live in love. You are love.

As a woman, I don't follow the male path. I don't see the need. Relationships are a part of life. Family and children are a part of life. Sex is a part of life. Where is the problem?

What you're saying points to a real difference in male and female spirituality. There are female teachers who say that life is the teacher. Just live a full life, live in a loving way, and that is enough. In a way, they are right. But that is generally not enough for the man. For the woman, if she has children and lives the householder path, it could be enough.

The beauty of such a path is that it is totally integrated, totally grounded. It sounds to me like a variation of the path of bhakti, of love, devotion and surrender. These come more naturally to the woman. Bernadette Roberts is an example of what is possible. (6)

Speaking without personal experience of what women should do for themselves distinct from men on a spiritual level, of what the wise women would call a good daily practice, I would still say women will benefit from Self-inquiry. To me it is the universal practice. Man or woman, you are the Self.

Speaking as a Tantrika, my view is that the mother's love is the glue that holds the human family together. Without it, human beings would have disappeared long ago. So, sure, do your living a loving life sadhana with family and all of that. Follow your heart.

Also do Self-inquiry. The two together is a beautiful path. Ultimately, the key is to keep investigating.

The sit-down Self-inquiry is honest deep investigation into the source of your existence. Love prepares the way for inquiry. Inquiry reveals the way to a deeper love. It is the cycle until the Self is revealed.

Listen to your heart. All the answers are in there. Male or female, the heart is the same, the heart is universal. The spiritual Heart has all the answers. As the Source of Love, the spiritual Heart is beyond the usual love. It is the very personal impersonal love. It is the ultimate of ultimates. It is the top state.

It is the supreme secret, but it is Silent. The great Love is everywhere, but it is quiet and invisible. As it moves there is the rustling of subtle leaves, of soft sweet yearning.

That is why you do not hear it. You must be inside of it. You must live on the inside of it. You cannot know it from outside. The word "courage" comes from the Latin "cor" meaning "heart." Be in your true "core." You can feel it in your heart right now. There is no victory without vulnerability. To conquer, you must be conquered by the Self.

Is it beneficial to be with someone who has realized the Self? And what is it like to be in a committed relationship or marriage if you are a realized person?

Relationships are no big deal either way. You can be married or not be married. Either way, it is the Self. When you are in an intimate relationship, that person is the Self. That person quite literally is you. All differences are superficial.

There is nothing special that you have to do. Your partner cannot interfere with your meditation. You ARE meditation and they are part of that. Life is an unbroken meditation.

You are THAT and they are a part of THAT. You could not separate them from your Self, from the Truth, even if you tried.

But you don't want it different. All the details, all the differences, all the nuances, all of it is the Self. All are adornments of the Self. The song of the sacred is found in the amazing everyday details.

To be in the Self is already the most intimate relationship that is possible. You are already living at the center of the most ultimate intimate connection. If you are living from here, you will not have difficulty loving them, but they may have a problem loving you. They will realize that you already love them more than they love themselves.

The sheer presence of your love, which is coming from the Self, will act upon them to expose their subsurface condemnation of the personal self. It is a paradox, for all that is offered is love, yet it can create earthquakes in their consciousness.

To love yourself totally and without conditions, in total forgiveness especially, and then to do the same with others, is very close to the truth of the Self. It is a path to the Self.

So in the end, what the other fears is real love. Living as the Self, that is what you bring to them. If they love love, then it will work out. But if they are afraid of love, of what it will reveal, then they are not ready. They will find an excuse to leave and move on.

The relationship challenges that come from being the Self with others is another story for another time. Suffice it to say that since you are being the Self, there is nothing else for you to do. It is their call. Mind you, if you are on the receiving end from someone who is living in the Self, then it is a great gift. Even so, the point is not them, it is you.

The point is your greatness as the Self, your potential for liberation. Love washes the false away, but it burns like acid for those who resist it. Love demands everything.

If you take the hint to love yourself totally and truly, and you go ahead and love your conventional self without limits, this love will itself begin to dissolve away all the obstacles. Even if you have not heard of enlightenment, washed in the cleansing cosmic waters of love without conditions or boundaries, the truth of who you are emerges.

Mother Nature Is Doing Everything

When years ago as a seeker I came across the exquisite empirical description of the state of non-doership in the *Bhagavad Gita*, I was astonished by it. It was poetry yet the author was most earnest in their assertion that they were describing authentic living.

Years later, when I finally came to understand for myself what was being described, I was astonished once again. Here was this document, a thousand or more years old, yet it was speaking to me with insights as fresh as the latest news at an Internet coffee house.

The deluded person thinks "I am the doer." The person who understands knows that it is the forces of Nature that do everything. In truth, the sage does nothing at all.

Lord Krishna explains this marker of enlightenment plainly and directly. It is a key piece of the eternal teaching. The notion of doership or agency is an empirical fact that people think they experience in their everyday lives. They believe they really are the doers in their lives and the creators of their lives. It this is true, it has vast spiritual implications.

If each individual is a unique independent doer, then God cannot be the ultimate power and absolute ruler. He has seven billion adolescent demigods with full free will running around doing as they wish on a fragile aging planet. Human beings either have the power to do their own thing or they don't. As long as an independent entity is assumed, as long as there is a ghost in the machine, the I-thought, there appears to be a strong dilemma.

On the other hand, if doership or agency is a superimposed belief due to identification of the mind with the physical body, this puts God back in charge. God is returned to His or Her proper status as absolute and total ruler of everyone and everything. If there is no real separate entity with free will and free choice, then there is no doership or agency either.

From my point of view, I don't see how people keep it going. I can't keep anything going. If it wants to go, then it goes. If it doesn't, then it doesn't.

I like to make myself coffee in the morning. Even though this happens just about every morning, I have no idea if it will happen the next morning. I have no idea if this world will be here or not. I have no idea who I will be or what I will want to do. I have no idea at all. So whatever happens, happens.

I'm used to this state of affairs now, but back when it started, I didn't believe it. So I came up with this thing I called the "Arm Test." I would sit on a chair and try to will one of my arms to rise. Nothing would happen. It is that way today. The body is spontaneous. No matter what the body does, I do not have the experience of doing it.

Is that scary? It sounds like you are being controlled by somebody else.

At first it was disconcerting, but I was never worried that anybody was controlling me. I knew instinctively that it was the action of the universe.

Besides, it's all brilliantly described in the *Bhagavad Gita*. You can't miss it. It's spelled out in black and white. I have nine different translations of the *Gita*. I love that book!

I don't think this non-doership will be a big selling point for people in the West. They want to go big and be in control. They want to be famous and make lots of money.

I agree. This is counter-intuitive as far as the average American is concerned. But if the so-called sage is just seeing the natural state, just seeing things the way they are, then what he is experiencing and seeing and feeling is the state for everybody, not just him.

I'm going to read Verses Eight and Nine from Chapter Five of the *Srimad Bhagavad Gita*. The translation by Swami Swarupananda is a good one. It holds up nicely compared to more recent versions. It dates from 1909 so it's in the public domain. (7)

Arjuna, being a man of action, a warrior, is confused. He is trying to understand what Krishna is talking about. They are having this conversation on a battlefield. If Arjuna does what Krishna is asking him to do, to fight, then he will be forced to kill some of his relatives. It is a family feud. There is a huge power struggle.

"The knower of Truth, being centered in the Self, thinks, 'I do nothing at all though seeing, hearing, touching, smelling, eating, going [to the bathroom], sleeping, breathing, speaking, letting go, holding, opening and closing the eyes. It is just the senses moving among the sense objects.'"

I still remember the first morning I woke up after the appearance of non-doership. My eyes blinked open on their own with a sudden dramatic "Pop!" It was a mild shock. When Krishna says that the correct view and way of thinking about our human actions is "I do nothing at all," he is describing the concrete scientific situation in everyday life.

After you are established in this condition, you cannot "do something" even if you try. I would conduct what I called my "Arm Experiment." I would try to move my arm as an act of autonomous will. There would be an electrical signal from my brain. I might even feel it in the arm. But the lifting of the arm did not take place. It got short-circuited.

The conventional doer sees a connection between thought and action that is not really there. To use the same example, he thinks that when he wills his arm to move and it moves, that proves that he has independent will and choice and he is the doer.

Krishna does not agree. Krishna is saying that the only reason it happened, the only way it could happen, is that God wills it.

Earlier in the *Bhagavad Gita*, Krishna says God (or Nature) is the doer, the only doer. This is in Chapter Three, Verses 27 and 28. (8)

"The Gunas [natural forces] of Prakriti [Nature] perform all action. With understanding deluded by egoism, man thinks, 'I am the doer.' But one with true insight into the domains of Guna and Karma [destiny], knowing that the Gunas as senses merely rest on [interact with] the Gunas as [sense] objects, does not become attached."

The implications of this view are profound. If thoughts do not cause action via the will power, thoughts can just come and go, actions can just come and go. Life is unbelievably simple and carefree. Life is spontaneous. Life is not what we think it is at all.

Even so, appropriate thoughts such as "I need to go to the store" may arise. But the experience of causality is not there. So the fact that the thought of going to the store arises does not mean that you will actually go to the store. The fact that you thought of going to the store did not cause you to go to the store.

If you do end up going to the store, or strictly speaking, the body ends up going to the store, it's because the body was compelled by Reality, by the world process, by God, to go to the store. The thoughts about doing that arose independently and coincidentally.

It is entirely possible for you to go to a store and not have planned it or thought about it. For example, you could be walking down the street, see an interesting store and go in.

This is how everything is happening for everybody, whether they know it or not, whether they have "realized" it or not. The world runs the world, not people. The world, as a function of Mother Nature, is in total command. Our bodies are Nature's servants, slaves, serfs, pawns, tools, devices and remote control robots.

The *Bhagavad Gita* says so. It says "Nature performs all actions." If you're confused, you think "I am the doer." If you're not confused, then you know you are not the doer. Nature is the doer.

The benefit of this correct understanding is true non-attachment, stable unshakeable inner peace. If you are not the doer, you can relax. Nothing is up to you.

The magnificent human body machine is the physical biocomputer. Our human brains are the sophisticated software. Mother Nature, the world process, is a cosmic super-computer that controls everything. The view "Nature performs all actions" is compatible with the new discoveries of modern science. It is a scientific view. Whether you believe in God or not, you can understand and appreciate that the forces of Nature are doing everything.

I have heard Advaita teachers say that because of non-doership, there is nothing you can do. There is nothing for you to do. Don't bother meditating, for example. Just be happy. They tell you that you can just "get it" and that's it. You are That anyway. Whatever you try to do will just get in the way. Your effort will just create problems. But I don't trust it.

I agree. It is taken out of context. The context of the Advaita position of don't do anything is when you're doing your sadhana with incredible focus and super-intensity and you're still having the experience of being the doer. That is what Krishna is talking about.

I think Krishna would laugh. "There is nothing you can do" is not the same as "There is nothing for you to do." People take it as the same. It is not!

You are the doer, so what are you going to do? That's our reality. It's not like Advaita students can choose to do work and take actions or not. Elsewhere in the *Gita*, Krishna is very clear about advocating action. He is not at all in favor of doing nothing.

The small self, the I-thought, holds onto this body identification for dear life. The way it is affirmed every day is that it remains firmly convinced that "I am the doer." Even when you understand this non-doership intellectually, it is not enough. All day long the world is reinforcing "You are the doer." This delusion is not easily overcome. You cannot just wish it away.

The advice "There is nothing you can do," that it doesn't matter what you do or don't do, is appropriate only for the very ripe student.

That person has seen for themselves the truth of Krishna's insight. Only they are not quite there yet. They have clearly seen the truth but the feeling of doership is still present. They still feel like the doer, like the agent. Yet they know they are not the doer.

They are on the verge. When my guru Ramesh Balsekar said those very words to me, "There is nothing you can do," I was ready. I was ripe. I was on the verge. But I had exhausted my search.

I had already tried everything. I already knew in my gut that he was right. There really was nothing "I," the separate little "I," could do. There was a lot that God and the Guru could do. That was not up to me. I already knew there was nothing I could do. I had tried!

But I could be prepared for Grace and I was prepared. My search was coming to an end one way or the other. It was my spiritual good fortune to meet an authentic guru when I was truly ready for him. By "ready" I mean I was at the end of my rope. I was toast.

You can do Self-inquiry under any and all circumstances, while you are active doing something or not doing anything. When you get to where the inquiry is automatic, you meet Krishna's requirements for the surrender of the fruits of your actions because now you are surrendering the one who would claim the fruits, the separate "I" that is identified with the body and claiming the body as itself. You are getting to the "True I" which is behind the false body-identified "I." When the claim for the body as the self stops, then the show is over. The I-thought throws in the towel. But it does not give up easily!

Can you see how if you stop identifying with the body, then the body can just function on its own? It does not need you to tell it what to do. It is taking direct orders straight from Nature's Central Headquarters, from the Cosmic Command Super Computer. Your mind was always an interloper, always in the way. You just did not know it. You do not need a mind.

I hope you don't take this the wrong way, but what you are talking about sounds a little bit like a horror movie, a zombie movie. They are very popular now. It is like all of us human beings are just zombies walking around. We are remote controlled robots. We think we are running the show but it's all a big game, a sneaky trick. God is chuckling to himself. We are his non-stop sit-com.

That's why I say you are already dead. There is nothing you can do about this situation. Like it or don't like it, it makes no difference. The world process is a universal machine. It just grinds on and on. You cannot stop it and you cannot change it. So you could say there is no hope. There is nothing to hope for.

No hope? That's sounds awfully dreary. Now I'm more depressed.

To the one who wants to stay in charge and be the doer, it is bad news. But if you are sick and tired of this world machine, and all of its crazy contradictions, and how it gives birth, maintains health and then mercilessly slaughters every living being, if you have had enough of that, then it is good news. It means you can get off the wheel. There is a way.

But it is not a source of hope. At the same time, though, it is offering you freedom from fear. No worries, mate. It's not in your hands anymore. Nothing to fear.

The secret hidden key is always found in the body identification. When that is dropped, then the non-doership automatically arises. To be the doer is just a trance, just hypnosis. When it is broken, you see it. It is obvious. But you must inquire until the very end.

Non-doership is an expression of the unbounded true Self, but it is not an end in itself. You can be in non-doership and still have lots of processing to do. It is not the end of the road. When you reach the Self, you will know it. You will not have questions anymore.

You can be in non-doership, and the mind will still have questions. You can still have major conflicts and confusion going on because the mind is not yet completely cleared up. It has not been nullified or eliminated.

Ramana once described the mind of the sage as being like the moon in the sky during the daytime. It is there, but it is not doing anything. Other times he said it is absolutely destroyed, just like it was never ever there.

It doesn't matter. The mind is the source of doubts and questions. When doubts and questions end, when you are at peace, then you are Home, in the Self. The wholeness is itself the answer. Thoughts can continue after the mind dies. Thoughts are not a problem.

When there is no mind, then they make no difference. But until then, thoughts are always tending to accumulate and turn from innocent little clouds into massive thunder clouds that send down thunderbolts and turn into big destructive tornadoes in a matter of seconds. So until the mind stops, vigilance must be maintained. Until the mind stops, until it finally grinds to a halt and shut downs, the tendency to create a false center exists.

After a certain point, you cannot do anything with any of this or about any of this. If a thought comes, it comes. If a thought stays, it stays. If a thought goes, it goes. If a thought seems to produce an action, then there is an action. But there is no cause and effect between thought and action. Thought and action are separate. This is high indifference.

If they arise at the same time, it is a connection of synchronicity or co-arising. It is not causality. If it was causality, then we could say the mind was causing the action. This is the same as saying that the mind is the doer, and we are back to being the body and the mind. Then we are back to being a body-identified doer. We are again the unconscious slave robot of the universal world machine, the Divine Mind Control of World Mother.

Either way, the body is her slave, her robot. The question is are you conscious of the truth or not. There is no mind. There is no doer. That's it. Now relax. Now let go. Just BE.

So we really are zombies! We are non-dual zombies! Grrrr.... *(Waves hands).*

Well, I don't experience it that way. I don't feel like a zombie. To me zombie implies a reduction in the quality of life. In fact, the outcome is the exact opposite. Your quality of life goes off the charts.

If you think you're the doer, and then you find out that you are not the doer, that is quite a shock. But you were never a zombie. Your ego, your I-thought, was already dead, but you didn't know it. When you realize that that is your real condition, then there is acceptance.

When you wake up to the nature of all this, after you work through the rough spots, it's actually even better. Now you get to feel the joy of being alive all of the time in every moment. You live from moment to moment in a state of total let-go.

You don't need to wait for a special high — to get drunk, to get high, to get laid, to get to the music show, to get to the movies, to get a raise, to get married, to get enlightened. This is freedom. It is not the same as happiness. It is beyond happiness. It is freedom.

So there is a "reward," you could say. This joy is the joy of being dead and knowing that you are dead. You are dead through and through. This uncaused spontaneous joy springs from the fact that your egocentric tendency to resist the moment to moment onslaught of the world process in your life is no longer arising.

You are no longer living in a state of non-stop resistance. No longer do you drive all day long with the brakes on. You have given up totally on controlling anything. All along, your resistance was futile. It was absolutely totally futile. You could never fight city hall. Now you know it and accept it.

Because you are truly dead, you truly don't care. Even this state of not caring is beyond your control. There is no greater indifference and peace than the indifference and peace of the dead.

If your surrender is total, permanent and final, then you can get the best of both worlds. You are dead while alive and alive while dead. You can have the silent peace of the still unmoving dead and the thrill of the fully alive.

Out of this unique combination freedom arises. Freedom is a feeling of being without limits as well as a "stateless state."

It is not just freedom from or freedom to. It is just pure freedom, like the smell of fresh mountain air. It is the taste, the smell, the flavor, the sound, the unspeakable indescribable joy of pure unadulterated unlimited being, of feeling absolutely free forever. All human beings aspire to be free. To be free is the highest of the high, it is the greatest of the great.

I will say it once again. You are already dead. Rejoice in this, for because of it, you can be free. You are already free. You are already dead. None of this is in your hands. Kali Ma has chopped off your head. You just don't know it yet. It has already happened!

Notes

(1) Sri Nisargadatta Maharaj, The Sense of "I am" (Consciousness), http://www.holybooks.com/wp-content/uploads/The-Sense-of-I-AM-Nisargadatta-Maharaj.pdf, accessed May, 2013.

Edited with excerpts from the three paragraphs of this one page document.

(2) Sri Ramana Maharshi Quotations, http://en.wikipedia.org/wiki/Ramana_Maharshi, accessed May, 2013.

Here are a handful of quotes from a Wikipedia article about the Heart and Self-inquiry.

(3) Sadhu Om and Michael James, http://www.happinessofbeing.com/The_Path_of_Sri_Ramana_Part_One.pdf, accessed May, 2013.

Part Two is also available as a free download. It is a different kind of approach. It with the devotional path of surrender.

(4) Harrigan, Joan Shivarpita. *Kundalini Vidya: the Science of Spiritual Transformation,* Patanjali Kundalini Yoga Care, Knoxville, TN, 2005.

(5) Paramahansa Yogananda, Autobiography of a Yogi (1946 edition), Chapter 30, http://www.holybooks.com/autobiogrphy-of-a-yogi-paramahansa-yogananda/, accessed May, 2013.

(6) Roberts, Bernadette. *The Experience of No-Self: A Contemplative Journey,* State University of New York Press, Albany, New York, 1994.

(7) Swami Swarupananda, Srimad Bhagavad Gita, 1909, http://www.sacred-texts.com/hin/sbg/sbg10.htm, accessed May, 2013.

(8) Swami Swarupananda, Srimad Bhagavad Gita, 1909, http://www.sacred-texts.com/hin/sbg/sbg08.htm#page_72, accessed May, 2013.

To receive a totally free copy of an excellent modern edition of the *Bhagavad Gita*, one of my very favorite translations, please go to this website: http://gita4free.com/

Mind-Blowing Books

These books have all played a pivotal role in my spiritual journey. I am deeply grateful to the authors for the help that they provided me. Their books and insights appeared when I needed them.

Balsekar, Ramesh. *Consciousness Speaks,* Advaita Press, Redondo Beach, CA, 1992.

Bhikku, Buddhadasa. *Anapanasati (Mindfulness of Breathing),* Sublime Life Mission, Bangkok, Thailand, 1980.

Buddhagosa, Bhadantacariya. *The Path of Purification (Visuddhimagga),* Buddhist Publication Society, Kandy, 1979.

Godman, David, Ed.. *Be As You Are: the Teachings of Sri Ramana Maharshi,* Penguin Books, London, England, 1985.

Godman, David and Sri Lakshmana Swamy. *No Mind, I Am the Self,* Sri Lakshmana Ashram, Nellore Dist. A. P. India, 2005.

Goel, B. S. *Psycho-Analysis and Meditation (The Theory and Practiuca of Psycho-Analytical Meditation),* Third Eye Foundation of India, Kurukshetra, Haryana, India, 1986. Note: This is a unique approach to deep psychological clearing via Kundalini meditation.

Harrigan, Joan Shivarpita. *Kundalini Vidya: the Science of Spiritual Transformation,* Patanjali Kundalini Yoga Care, Knoxville, TN, 2005.

Kaufman, Barry Neil. *To Love Is to Be Happy With,* Ballantine Books, New York, NY, 1977.

Klein, Jean. *I Am,* Third Millenium Publications, St. Peter Port, Guernsey, C. I., 1989.

Maharaj, Nisargadatta. *I Am That,* Acorn Press, Durham, NC, 1990.

Maharaj, Siddharameshwar. *Amrut Laya (The Stateless State),* Shri Sadguru Siddharameshwar Adhyatma Kendra, Mumbai, India, 2000. Note: Includes brilliant "Master Key to Self-Realization."

Maharishi, Mahesh Yogi. *Maharishi Mahesh Yogi On The Bhagavad Gita: A New Translation and Commentary Chapters 1-6,* Penguin Books, Baltimore, MD, 1972.

Maharshi, Ramana. *Talks with Sri Ramana Maharshi,* Sri Ramanasramam, Tiruvannamalai, India, Sixth Edition, 1978.

Nikhilananda, Swami. *Gospel of Sri Ramakrishna,* Ramakrishna-Vivekananda Center, New York, NY, 1984.

Ramana, A. *Consciousness Being Itself,* AHAM Publications, Asheboro, NC, 1995.

Ram Das, Swami. *In Quest of God,* Ananadashram, Kerala, India.

Rinpoche, Namgyal. *Body, Speech & Mind,* Bodhi Publishing, Kinmount, Ontario, Canada, 2004.

Roberts, Bernadette. *The Experience of No-Self: A Contemplative Journey,* State University of New York Press, Albany, NY, 1994.

Suzuki, Shunryu. *Zen Mind, Beginner's Mind.* Weatherhill, New York, NY, 1973.

Sadhu Om. Sri. *Path of Sri Ramana Maharshi, Part One,* Sri Ramana Kshetra, Tiruvannamalai, India, 2005.

Sayadaw, Mahasi. *The Progress of Insight: A Treatise on Buddhist Satipatthana Meditation,* Buddhist Publication Society, Sri Lanka, 1998.

Shankaracharya, Sri and Swami Turiyananda, Translator. *Viveka-Chudamani,* Sri Ramakrishna Math, India.

Trungpa, Chogyam. *Cutting Through Spiritual Materialism,* Shambhala, Boston, MA, 1987.

Tulku, Tarthang. *Hidden Mind of Freedom,* Dharma Publishing, Berkeley, CA, 1981.

Venkatesananda, Swami. *The Concise Yoga Vasistha,* State University of New York Press; Albany, NY, 1984.

Venkataramiah, Mungala. *Tripura Rahasya: The Mystery beyond the Trinity,* Sri Ramanasramam, Tiruvannamalai, India, 2006.

Yogananda, Paramahansa. *Autobiography of a Yogi,* Self-Realization Fellowship, Los Angeles, CA, 1998.

Yogeshwaranand Saraswati, Swami. *Science of Soul (Atma-Vijnana),* Yog Niketan Trust, Rishikesh, Indai, 1974.

Zen Master Seung Sahn and Stephen Mitchell. *Dropping Ashes on the Buddha: The Teachings of Zen Master Seung Sahn,* Grove Press, New York, NY, 1994.

Meet the Author

RAMAJI

Ramaji teaches Advaita and non-duality in the San Diego, California area. He has been a devotee of Kali Ma since She spoke to him at the Hollywood Vedanta Society Temple in 1982. He is easily reached via email or his web site Ramaji.org.

Ramaji works with students all over the world via email and Skype. He currently has students in Australia, Thailand, United Kingdom, Brazil, Japan, India, Canada and the United States.

Although there is a small fee for the RASA transmission, the personal spiritual coaching and ongoing non-dual dialog he provides to his students is offered on a love donation basis.

He teaches Self-inquiry in the tradition of Ramana Maharshi with a non-dual Tantra and Kundalini twist.

His work includes guiding students in the investigation of the arising I-thought, stabilization in the thought-free state, revelation of the Heart on the right and illumination of the Amrita Nadi.

Ramaji also provides support for people on a devotional path with Divine Mother, Kali Ma devotees especially, and for awakening Kundalini experiencers.

Via telephone, Skype or in person, he offers RASA (Ramaji Advaita Shaktipat Attunement). This attunement opens the Crown chakra to Divine Mother's gentle descending Grace for rapid awakening of enlightenment. Some experience this radiant spiritual download as a white or golden light.

As the Crown chakra opens, identification with the physical body is reduced. A brightly glowing wide open Crown chakra is characteristic of an enlightened person. It is a sign that body identification has been dropped.

Many Blessings in the One Supreme Self,
RAMAJI

Ramaji.org

Meetup.com/Ramaji-Satsang-Group/ (local San Diego meetings)

YouTube Channel: Ramaji Satsang

Email: satsangwithramaji@gmail.com

Made in the USA
Lexington, KY
17 February 2018